Open Windows

On Times And Places And Hopes For Peace

Open Windows

On Times And Places And Hopes For Peace

John S. Workman

With Sally Crisp

August House / Little Rock
P U B L I S H E R S

©Copyright 1988 by John S. Workman
All rights reserved. This book, or parts thereof,
may not be reproduced in any form without
permission.
Published by August House, Inc.,
P.O. Box 3223, Little Rock, Arkansas, 72203,
501-663-7300.

Printed in the United States of America

10 9 8 7 6 5 4 3 2 1

LIBRARY OF CONGRESS CATALOGING-IN-PUBLICATION DATA
Workman, John S., 1927-
Open windows: of times and places and hopes for
peace / by John
S. Workman; edited by Sally Crisp.
p.   cm.
ISBN 0-87483-074-5: $8.95
1. Meditations. 2. Workman, John S., 1927- .
I. Crisp, Sally.
II. Title.
BV4832.2.W685 1988   88-24115
242—dc19   CIP

First Edition, 1988

Cover illustration by Bill Jennings
Production artwork by Ira Hocut
Typography by Diversified Graphics, Little Rock, AR
Design direction by Ted Parkhurst
Project direction by Hope Norman Coulter

This book is printed on archival-quality paper which
meets the guidelines for performance and durability of
the Committee on Production Guidelines for Book
Longevity of the Council on Library Resources.

AUGUST HOUSE, INC.   PUBLISHERS   LITTLE ROCK

To my mother, Meta Sue Sparks Workman, and to the memory of my father, James W. Workman.

Thanks for loving each of your three children enough to let us learn about open windows.

And thanks for showing us, through your own faith and courage and love, that God watches over all the world's Open Window children.

Acknowledgments

With appreciation to all those open-window people who, by their example, have shown me that life is an adventure, a marvel, a miracle that must never be shut out.

With love and appreciation to my wife, Liz, whose own openness to life and passion for justice and peace has opened to me so many windows of learning, compassion, and inspiration. Thank you, Liz, for encouraging us both to keep the windows open, though it often would have been easier, more comfortable, safer, to live closed-window lives.

With thanks and much love to our children, John, Steve, Susie, and Chuck, for being gutsy enough to live your own open-window lives. Wonderful!

And with appreciation to Sally Chandler Crisp, another open-windows person, whose editorial skills have made possible this volume and its predecessor, *Fireflies in a Fruit Jar*. Thanks, Sally.

JSW

I want to say "thank you" to the following people who have helped this book come into being: Huey and Molly Crisp, Lucille Chandler Bryson, Pat Caffey, Sandie Jacobi, Matt Nagle, Catherine Branton, Palla Smith, Veneta Hines, Kathy Juniper, Barry Maid, Charles Anderson, and especially Hope Coulter, Ted and Liz Parkhurst, and John Workman.

With love,
SCC

About the Author

A fifth-generation Methodist clergyman, John S. Workman was educated at Hendrix College in Conway, Arkansas, and Perkins School of Theology in Dallas, Texas. After serving in the U.S. Army Security Agency in Japan and Korea, he served churches in Oil Trough, Sylvan Hills, Berryville, Cabot, and Little Rock, Arkansas. Formerly editor of the *Arkansas Methodist* newspaper, he has contributed to many journals and magazines and is the author of *Fireflies in a Fruit Jar*. He is currently religion editor of the *Arkansas Gazette*.

About the Editor

Sally Crisp has been the director of the Writing Center at the University of Arkansas at Little Rock since 1981 and has taught writing at the college level since 1972. The editor of *Fireflies in a Fruit Jar*, she lives in Little Rock with her husband and two daughters.

Contents

Acknowledgments   7

Introduction   11

Ruminations   13

Destinations   33

Avocations   53

Vocations   91

Explorations   111

Peregrinations   131

Introduction

Sights, sounds, smells, and refreshing breezes—all these flow in and out of an open window . . . Most of us open our windows rarely, if at all, any more, but an open window still makes a useful metaphor. In this book, John Workman encourages us to be "open windows" to each other (and ourselves), to times and places, to the possibilities of God's peace. In the open windows metaphor we may even hear an echo of the prayer of St. Francis: "Make me a channel of Your peace."

The open windows metaphor is John's. I'll let you discover all he does with it. But since I have named this book, it is mine as well. Let me elaborate. I think you'll find that in his writing John Workman has been—is—an open window himself. In these pieces, you will see him opening himself to the world, with its pain, sorrow, joy, and beauty, bringing the world into himself—and out again to us. He seems to me relatively unafraid of people, of strange places, other times, life's experiences. (As we know, fear and isolation can close windows.)

And just as he travels out into the wide world and various experiences, likewise John travels inside himself and lets us see something of his inner world. But he doesn't travel inward as some writers have, egotistically assuming our interest; instead he makes meaning of his inner feelings and foibles—for reflection and for fun. And whether he takes us outside or inside, we feel we know him, and often we feel a refreshing breeze. So

11

in part my metaphor is this: John as an open window to God's world and to us, to himself and to us.

But, even with many stories to tell, John remains only one, however open. So, windows? In my metaphor making, you and I are the others implied in windows— for it takes all of us to make *Open Windows.*

So join me, won't you, join us, John and me, for this open windows experience and in this petition: *Make us open windows, Lord, to You, ourselves, each other, Your peace.*

. . . Feel the breeze?

Sally Chandler Crisp
June 1988

Ruminations

In Praise of Open Windows

I suppose it's a call back to an earlier childhood. Back to when I used to lie awake on summer evenings and, through open windows, hear the outdoor sounds of the dark and watch the moonlight make dancing shadows on the window curtains moving gently in the cool night breeze.

But whatever the reason, I am a late turner-oner of the air conditioning in the spring and summer. I like to keep the windows open just as long as the temperature will allow before I give in and pull them down and turn on the artificial air and hear its monotonous, unimaginative sound.

With my windows open I can tell what my bobwhites are doing and what my cricket friends have to say. And I can know when my dog comes out of her house, just below my study window, to make her midnight inspection before returning to sleep on her other side for a while. And I can hear, while falling peacefully to sleep, the beautiful lullaby of the wind in my pine trees and listen as it rustles the leaves on the big oak, my old friend of many conversations.

I miss my outdoor sounds when the season finally forces me to join the civilized world again and shut out all these wonders.

So I like my open-windows way. I like it in my house and I like it that way in my head and my heart. I like to hear and join the laughter and celebrating and the joy and the peace. And, too, I "like" to share the crying and the sorrow and the grief and the pain of our world. For only by doing so are we really alive. And only so may we begin our response to it all, to give what we have to give and receive what is given to us.

It occurs to me that Christians should be "open window" people.

Don't Mess Around with My Religion

You are not going to like this column.

This column is going to make you mad.

What you're about to read is guaranteed to spoil your day and quite possibly mess up your whole New Year.

If you don't want your blood pressure agitated and possibly your whole life ruined, don't read any further. Quit now while there is time.

If you're still with us, relax. We're just trying to make a point: most of us don't like to be disturbed (though we are curious enough, as in the current instance, to wonder what's happenin' when some doomsayer carries on about all the turmoil to come).

Our point is that we humans don't like to be upset. We like peace and quiet. We don't want our ideas challenged. We don't want nobody messin' around with our religion.

The thoughts are not untimely at the beginning of a New Year when, hopefully, we are open to pondering, meditating, and entertaining—at least for a few moments, anyway—some new ideas.

Ah, yes—new ideas. That's where the rub comes in regarding religion. For a lot of people, religion and new ideas don't mix. Oil and water. Apples and oranges.

But hold on. If we recall correctly, new ideas are a lot of what the Bible and the gospel are all about. They talk quite a bit about being strangers and sojourners in a foreign land, searching for the city whose builder and maker is God, venturing forth on faith and taking risks and such as that. The Bible and the gospel have something to say about our shaking loose from old ways and running the risk of taking up new ways.

But that kind of stuff leaves us uneasy. We don't like to let go of the familiar, which gives us security.

We've a friend, a preacher, who tells about an old

tree-trimmer who was asked how he could work high in a tree and swing from limb to limb with such confidence while suspended only by a thin rope.

"You just have to learn how to let go without turnin' loose," the old tree-trimmer said.

My friend the preacher said he found the thought especially helpful to families who had lost loved ones. The image also is relevant to the coming of a year which confronts us with all sorts of newness, uncertainty, and risk.

Perhaps life consists of learning to let go while hanging on.

And perhaps it's not a too far-fetched interpretation of the biblical message to say it's okay to be edgy about the unknown—just so long as we remember that the rope that's holding this old world is tied securely.

On Being Totally Irrelevant

Most folks don't need to be encouraged in this respect, but there is a sense in which one of the marks of a civilized person is the ability to be totally oblivious—for a time, anyway—to whatever is going on. To be completely unaware of what's happening. To be totally irrelevant.

That comment, admittedly facetious, is not intended as counsel for a way of life. It is, rather, a suggestion for occasional indulgence in an exercise that is vital to the maintenance of good mental health, especially in these hectic times.

Hence, a recommendation, a prescription if you will, for use during the coming weeks of spring: whenever the opportunity affords, listen to thunder. That's right—listen to spring thunder.

Thunder at any time of year is a marvel to behold. It is an event, a grand happening, one of creation's most exciting gifts. Thunder is perhaps one of the most unsung of all nature's wonders. It deserves better press. And spring thunder is thunder at its best. Let all the people praise thunder.

Spring thunder is the hands-down winner in any thunder competition. It is louder than the thunders all the other seasons can offer. It is more sudden, more abrupt. When accompanied by lightning, another of the sky's grand gifts, spring thunder's loud report can make the most reluctant jump, giving lessons in promptness no other teacher can equal.

And spring thunder is more prolonged than its competitors. Its rumblings can ramble on and on for delightful distances. One can trace its wanderings from one county to the next, can hear it bounce around among the mountains, roll down the valleys, slide across the flatlands, and disappear somewhere off beyond the horizon, waiting for another chance to be born again.

Perhaps one of the strange attractions of thunder is that it is one of the few sounds in this noise-filled world that is still nature's own. In a time when human beings have caused so many deafening noises, it is refreshing to be surprised by sounds we haven't created, ones we have nothing to do with, over which we have no control and that we cannot predict or muffle.

The glory of thunder may be that it is an audible, awesome reminder that there is still One who is beyond, One who is totally "other," One who is completely majestic.

If it is true, as Proverbs suggests, that there is purpose in all things, thunder has its reasons. Who knows what mulchings it does for the soil, what loosenings it works in the soul? Who knows what dormant, sluggish chords thunder may awaken within us, what unsounded chimes it may strike in our hearts and heads?

Those who make time to be "totally irrelevant," by doing such things as listening to spring thunder, may be best equipped to analyze and interpret—and perhaps to redirect—those sounds and silences that human beings have inflicted upon this planet.

Last Days of August

I live across the street from a public school, and I've noticed that things over there have been picking up during the last couple of weeks.

Although it's been quiet all summer, these last days of August are showing signs of things to come.

Work crews have been sprucing up the lawn, others have been cleaning rooms and waxing floors and doing a bunch of other stuff—I can't really figure out just what.

Down the block, the junior high football squad is well into the second week of its preschool "two-a-days," a sure sign that summer's hours are numbered and fall is sneaking up on us, however quietly.

Before you know it, the advance troops—that gallant cadre of teachers—will be there to begin plotting whatever it is that they plot when, a week before the deluge, they go to their rooms early and stay late.

Let's hope they're up to some good.

What all these people don't know is how all this activity affects us alumni. (It so happens that the very first school I ever entered, as a trembling first-grader, was on these very grounds, though that building has long ago gone the way of all old school buildings.)

You put all this together—getting school buildings ready, football practice, the aroma of floor wax, seeing an occasional teacher with that "I'm-ready-for-'em" look written all over her, and TV weatherpersons making guarded predictions about a coming change in the weather—put all that together and it's easy for an older person to get the sillies.

Like, for instance, it's easy under such circumstances for older persons to corner anybody they can find and talk on and on about how they remember, way back yonder, the last barefoot days of summer.

Such older people want to find somebody—anybody —to tell how terrible it was to have to say goodbye to bare feet, short pants, swimmin' holes, ice-cold lemonade, and long, lazy summer days. They want to talk about how they hated to put on those hot school clothes and spend five whole days in a row inside a building studying books.

So, here's some free advice: stay away from older people during these last few days of August.

But perhaps it's just as well. Older people need a last-days-of-August ritual, too. Such times remind us that life goes on, that life is good, and that there just might be something that all of us—older people and young people alike—can do to help each other along the way.

Your assignment for today: say a prayer for our school youngsters—and for our teachers, administrators, and staff people. They've got a big job ahead of them.

God bless them all.

Waiting for Fall

It occurred to us the other day, while waiting for fall to arrive, that we human beings consume a lot of time waiting for things to happen.

We wait for summer to be over. We wait for the kids to grow up. We wait for fall to come. We wait for the "big break" in our careers. We wait for our ship to come in. We wait for spring to arrive.

How, we asked ourself on the week's last day of summer (as we watched and waited patiently for a leaf on our maple tree to change color), can one justify all that time spent waiting?

Good question, we said to ourself as we settled further into our patio chair. We'll have to sit here a spell and think about that.

Just suppose, we thought, that one could repossess all the world's wasted time—that one could redeem all the hours and minutes that careless folks have frittered away since the beginning of the ages! How much time could we collect, do you suppose?

Hmmm. We'll have to think about that for a while.

And whatever happened, do you suppose, to our hummingbirds? They haven't been around for more than a week. Hmmm again. Maybe we ought to sit here a bit to see if they'll come back and get just one more gulp, at least, of this nourishing red sugarwater before they fly off to spend the winter in Mexico or wherever (if indeed that's really what they do).

But you know something? Just suppose we really could redeem all the world's wasted time. Then we'd have another problem on our hands: what to do with it all. (And besides, who knows—recycled time might not be as good as the original stuff. Using second-hand time might be like buying a used car—you'd likely end up getting somebody else's problems.)

Oh, well, maybe fall, which was supposed to have arrived Tuesday (wasn't it?), will get here tomorrow. Or maybe Wednesday. We'll see.

But enough of this.

We submit that there's a difference between wasting time and waiting for something to happen. It's probably a sin to really "waste" time. But we've a theory: it's very difficult to actually waste time (though we know some experts at trying).

Authentic "waiting" can be a blessing, an experience in which one is granted glimpses into the mysteries and

21

marvels of the universe.

Time can be wasted. It also can be invested.

We'll let you think about all this stuff for awhile. We've got some more season-watching to do.

Empty Coffee Cans

Show us a person who throws away empty coffee cans and we'll show you a person who doesn't appreciate the really finer things in life.

That's a tough indictment, we know, but we believe we can make it stick.

There's something basically wrong, perhaps even immoral, about throwing away perfectly good coffee cans. There ought to be a bunch of federal troops—yea, an international brigade—on constant standby, ready to apprehend people who throw away empty coffee cans.

Those of us who hoard old coffee cans suffer considerable abuse for our peculiarity. We're always being ridiculed.

"What in the world are you ever going to do with all those old coffee cans?" is the kind of stuff we have to put up with. Our theory: anyone who has to ask that question isn't capable of comprehending our specialness.

There are two kinds of people in the world—those who save old coffee cans and those who throw them away. We believe we know which of those people God loves best.

The subject is, of course (you guessed it) a religious one, swarming with all sorts of theological dimensions. Regretfully, we've space for only the briefest commentary.

There is no such thing as "a mere coffee can." The sentence "It's just an old coffee can" should be outlawed in the English language and all other civilized tongues.

An empty coffee can is a joy forever.

An empty coffee can is an invitation to imagine, to plan, to dream.

An empty coffee can is a symbol of trust in the future, of treasures to be safely stored away.

One never knows, now does one, when an empty coffee can will be needed. Just think of all the things one can keep in those little gems!

One can easily imagine that the Pearl of Great Price was kept safe in an empty coffee can.

We're prepared to play hardball on this matter. Remember the great depression of 1929? Recall our most recent Black Market Monday of last October? Ah ha! But have you ever heard of the crash of this world's coffee can banks? Of course you haven't.

Coffee can savers are born, not made. As children, they were the little boys and girls who daydreamed a lot, whose mothers couldn't get them to come in for supper, who built treehouses, who swam in swimmin' holes, and who ordered secret decoder rings from the back of cereal boxes.

Most of them grew up to become Democrats and almost all were successful in life.

Maybe a psychiatrist or one of those kinds of people could figure it out. I don't know. But there's something reassuring about having a bunch of empty coffee cans around.

But whatever, be kind to empty coffee can hoarders. God, who found dandy uses for a lot of ordinary things—such as a couple of old stone tablets and an empty manger—has a special understanding of such folks.

Be Not Too Hasty

For any who may think that Christmas is over with, this reminder: according to an ancient tradition, Christmas has, in fact, just begun. What we've been celebrating for the last four weeks has been Advent, a time of anticipation and preparation.

But now, with Christmas Day 1987 an accomplished fact, we enter what some consider the *real* celebration of Christmas—the Twelve Days of Christmas. These days, from Christmas Day through Epiphany (January 6), commemorate the Wise Men's journey to find the baby Jesus. That visit has been considered an affirmation of the divinity of the Christ Child.

So do not be too hasty in bidding Christmas farewell. These Twelve Days afford a grand opportunity to ponder the wonder and mystery of the Incarnation.

There is another dimension to this week that begins with Christmas Day. These days between Christmas Day and New Year's Day might be called "the in-between week."

This in-between week is perhaps the most unusual week of the entire year. It is different from any other week in all the preceding twelve months.

This week is one in which our regular schedules and activities are put on hold. It's a slowing-down week, a coasting week, a wrapping-up week.

This is the week when we make our formal ending of society's triple-header holiday season—those festive days that begin with Thanksgiving, peak with Christmas and Hanukkah, and are concluded with all the emotions that attend the ending of one year and the beginning of the next.

Certainly there is no week like this in-between week.

It is time for memories. It is a mellow time.

It is a time of joy and sorrow, laughter and tears,

24

regrets and resolutions.

It is a time for forgiving and asking for forgiveness. It is a time for peacemaking. It is a time for loving and being loved.

It is a time for solitude, for being quiet. It is a time for contemplation. It is a time to think and to refrain from thinking.

It is a time to put haste aside for awhile. It is a time to be still, to sleep, to dream, to wake.

It is a time to be open to the future, a time for planning.

It is a time for collective celebrations, when congregations gather in joyous, triumphant worship. It is a time for shouting from the housetops.

Surely this in-between week is one of God's grand gifts.

So enjoy this day and the remainder of the journey with the Wise Men. Follow the star.

And after that, prepare to shift gears. The New Year will be here.

A happy in-between week to one and all!

The Dangerous Season

We hate to disturb your sleep, but you need to know something. We've entered the dangerous season.

That's right—the dangerous season.

How so, you ask?

This will take some explaining, so stay with us.

The dangerous season, you see, results from a combination of factors: falling temperatures outdoors; rising temperatures indoors; pajamas made mostly of polyester fabrics; and bedcovers constructed from other manmade materials.

That makes a dangerous season?

You bet it does. Bear with us a bit longer.

That combination of factors was responsible for my very near premature demise the other evening. It happened this way.

I retired early on a cold night when the humidity was particularly low and our furnace had made the inside air especially dry. The first hint of trouble came when I, clad in my mostly polyester pajamas, turned off the bedroom light, scooted across our million-kilowatt carpet, jumped into bed, and quickly pulled up the bedcovers (also of man-made materials).

Holy smoke! Sparks flew all over the place. The friction generated by all those man-made fabrics, in the hot and dry air, precipitated a veritable Fourth of July celebration. It's a wonder our smoke alarm didn't go off. The light show continued throughout the night, little explosions popping each time I turned over and ruffled the covers.

Imagine the embarrassment of trying to explain how a loved one was suddenly summoned under such circumstances. It's not a pleasant thought.

You probably haven't caught it yet, but the topic has definite religious dimensions. Dangerous seasons are always lurking nearby, seeking to entrap the unwary pilgrim.

An example is at hand. These post-Christmas and post-Hanukkah days can be an especially dangerous season for the well-intentioned faithful.

That danger: the tendency, prevalent in our wildly secularized society, to get back to our business-as-usual ways just as soon as the glow from our religious holidays has dimmed.

It's an old danger, of course, one that confronted even the Prophets and the Wise Men.

So be forewarned. The world's bright lights can, unless we're careful, blind us to the continuing twinkle of Bethlehem's star and Hanukkah's glowing message of religious freedom.

These are important days, these days following our holy seasons. Let's not let the flashy distractions of the world blind us to their specialness.

Be careful out there. Things can go *poof* at any moment.

Yesterday

It is wonderful to think of yesterday.

It is a delight to recall the past.

It is a joy to relive old memories, to recall half-forgotten experiences, to clothe them again with names and faces and sounds and colors.

Yesterday is a treasure, a gem to be set with care. Yesterday is an old friend, to be visited as opportunity affords. Yesterday is a winter fireside companion, a summer patio chum.

It is true, of course, that not all our yesterdays are enjoyable. Some of our past days are better forgotten, hidden where we need not look upon them again.

But most of us would suffer the harsh remembrance of pain or sorrow or guilt or fault or failure for the joy of recalling those other yesterdays, the grand ones.

So our thought for the day is a memory, a recollection of days which, though long gone by, seem almost as yesterday.

It was a small front yard—some grass, a tree, much dust—in the same town in which I now make my home, Conway, Arkansas. Our family lived here during my early childhood.

I don't remember the year nor do I know how old I was, though it must have been in the 1930s and I about age five.

The date is uncertain, but in my head and heart the scene remains constant, though now a faded tintype, edges worn and crumbly with decades of handling.

It was the front yard at our Methodist parsonage home, on Center Street. The occasion must have been one of many—my older brother and I playing with little pot-metal toy cars at the base of what I recall as a tall tree in our front yard. (Although the house and tree still stand this half-century or more later, both seem not nearly so large as recalled in memory).

I remember the hot summer dust in which we played. I remember the little stick houses and car garages we built with twigs that fell from the tree limbs above.

I recall the childhood joy of imagining my little car climbing the steep, rough mountain roads we built around the roots of the tree, roots exposed above the earth.

I remember the aromas and sensations of summer— honeysuckle in the sun, hot dust under bare feet, cool moss to lie upon on the north side of the wood-frame house.

I remember the sights and sounds of July and August—billowy white clouds against a robin's-egg-blue sky; giant thunderheads moving in from the west, stacked up on top of each other, towering to heaven itself and announcing their soon-coming with faint rumblings that shook the heavy air.

Even now when I hear distant thunder it is those scenes, those days, that place—that front yard and that tree—that I recall.

I recently heard an artist/theologian say that the tree is an especially significant symbol in our memories.

Trees, like mountains, are so much more than they are. They are symbols of life and growth. They speak eloquently of strength and charm and loveliness and mystery. Trees are a promise of the future.

The sound of wind in a tree can be both a lullaby and an alarm, singing us to sleep or calling us to wake and be alert.

Blessed be the trees.
Blessed be our memories.

I've often wondered why this particular memory is among the first I can recall. There doesn't seem to be any special meaning in it, any hidden philosophical significance. It's just a memory. And that, perhaps, is what makes it so special indeed.

Tomorrow

If yesterday is a delight and a joy to recall, then surely tomorrow is a wonder and a prize to cherish.

Tomorrow is anticipation. Tomorrow is a brightly-wrapped present, an excitement-filled mystery with our name on it.

Tomorrow!

What a grand word. What a marvelous prospect.

Who cares that tomorrow never really comes? It is enough that it is there.

Tomorrow is our dreamer, our visionary, our planner. Tomorrow is our counselor, our priest, our redeemer. Tomorrow is our savior.

If it were not for tomorrow, life would lose its mystery and mourning would possess us all.

It is about tomorrow that we dream today. It is for tomorrow that all our yesterdays and todays exist.

Tomorrow is our mother and our father. Tomorrow is our hope-giver.

Tomorrow blesses us with the excitement of the unknown.

Tomorrow, your name is future. What price may be put upon your gift?

Today

Beware, all you who sing the praises only of yesterday and tomorrow.

Beware, for you face a grave danger. You stand in peril of missing the most grand treasure of all.

Today!

Aye, today.

Yesterday can be a robber and tomorrow a fickle suitor. To our yesterdays, today is unknown; to our tomorrows, today is an irrelevant stranger.

Today is one's most grand possession, one's ultimate treasure. It is today alone—this very moment; not yesterday and not tomorrow—in which one may truly, and in fact, live.

Only today—only in the present moment—may one waste or spend time, may one invest or squander the minutes, may one marvel at the mystery of time or allow it to pass without its due tribute and praise.

Though today may hold dear memories and tomorrow be the place of fondest dreams, it is today that is the ultimate gift.

Guard today well—but not too well, lest in the guarding you fail to live.

Today is worth whatever risk may be required to discover its wonders, its sweetest secrets, its most grand gifts, and its finest joys.

Use today wisely, but do not miss the chance to play the fool (for fools, sometimes, are the true wise ones among us).

Make today your best friend.

Revel in today! Spend today lavishly. It is the true Pearl of Great Price.

Time like a River

Someone once said that time is like a river. As one who's been dunked for a half-dozen decades now, I agree.

Time, like a river, moves unremittingly toward its goal.

Time, like a river, gathers speed as it pursues its course.

Time, like a river, collects more baggage as it makes its voyage.

Time, like a river, grows more impatient as it nears its final home.

Time, like a river, defies those who would restrain it, change it, turn it around.

And Time, like a river, laughs at our attempts to define it with mere words. Time winks at those who would say that Time is like a river.

Nevertheless, Time *is* like a river.

Time has her moods.

Time is a fickle suitor.

Time can be calm or stormy, gently or tough, tranquil or tempestuous, quiet or deafening, cantankerous or cooperative.

Time has her own mind.

Time is one of the few true rulers of the universe.

Time is answerable only to the Master Timekeeper.

As a veteran Time-traveler, I've had some truck with this most persistent, yet elusive, of teasers. Thoughts of Time have, of late, rested both more heavily and more lightly upon my heart.

Time can be both a friend and an adversary, even an enemy. Time can be a joy (ask the person who is happy), or Time can be a burden (ask the person who tosses on a bed of pain).

Time, old chum, you are a paradox, a mystery.

Where do you go, Time, when you finally run out in the sea?

What kind of home do you sleep in when your river-bed has worn thin?

What kind of noise do you make when your last cascading torrent has been sucked up by the sun? What kind of wetness do you have when all that is left of your travels is dust?

If it is true, Time, that you are like a river, won't you grant me one wish?

Won't you promise you'll always keep rolling—even though I may not hear your marvelous, peaceful, frightening, ever-enticing sounds?

Destinations

On Sleeping Soundly

Having just recently returned from a twelve-day trip to three Central American countries—Nicaragua, Honduras, and El Salvador—I think some reflections on the experience may be in order.

When Americans travel abroad, especially in these troubled times, perhaps the most common reaction upon returning to the United States is "My, it's great to be back in the land of the free! What a wonderful country we live in—I wouldn't want to be anywhere else in the world!"

Those are understandable, honest expressions. Given the kind of tensions, poverty, limitations on human rights, and other problems that people in so many other parts of the world must endure these days, those who benefit from the freedoms of this great country and enjoy its spiritual and material blessings have reasons aplenty to be grateful.

But there is an unbecoming edge to those kind of comments. Without intention, such statements can carry "ugly American" connotations. They can convey an uncomplimentary "lifeboat mentality"—"We're lucky to be in the lifeboat during this terrible storm and we're going to make darn sure we stay here and that nobody gets our place!"

For the people of the biblical faiths—which are international and defy man-made barriers—that kind of thinking is unacceptable. It is right and proper for United States citizens to be grateful and proud of their freedoms and blessings. But there is something terribly wrong when that pride and gratitude degenerate to a selfish apartness that makes Americans insensitive to the sufferings and needs of others and undisturbed by the injustices that so often contribute to those conditions.

Two major impressions, each contradictory of the other, linger after my traveling for almost two weeks in deeply troubled Central America: the reality of fear among so many people, and the bold determination, in spite of that fear, to find a better way.

One experience especially reflects the fear: among the several score of persons interviewed or met, almost two-thirds insisted they not be identified in newspaper reports dealing with political or social—or even religious—issues in their country.

It became a common experience, especially in Nicaragua and El Salvador, to speak daily with people who feared for their lives.

Numerous experiences reflect the determination to find a better way. Two examples only: a young lawyer, the head of the legal department of El Salvador's Human Rights Commission, who in spite of repeated threats on his life persists in efforts to do something about the horrible atrocities that continue daily to afflict his people; and the pastor and members of a small Lutheran congregation who are determined, even at no small risk to their personal safety, to give Christian ministry to refugees.

It is good to be able to come home to the United States of America. It is not so good to realize that one can learn again so quickly how to sleep soundly at night while knowing that multitudes of people, not so far away, are afraid to close their eyes.

Once to Africa

I recall the photograph, a sweeping, breathtaking panorama.

In the distance was a vast, snow-covered mountain range, partly hidden by clouds but with a towering summit commanding the horizon. In the foreground was a lonely, serene lake, surrounded by giant evergreen trees.

Beneath this photo was the promotional message, as I recall it: "Once you've been to Alaska, you can never come all the way home."

Marvelous!

The thought has stayed with me—not regarding Alaska (I've never been there, I'm sorry to say), but regarding another distant place.

Africa.

Though I traveled to Africa long ago, my experience with that far continent has been the same. Once you've been to Africa, you can never come all the way home.

It's strange, regarding Africa. Although my travels there date back more than a dozen years—a three-week trip in 1975 and two years later a six-week journey that took me to six countries on the continent—I have never been able to shake Africa out of my mind and heart.

Although the two trips produced a bunch of articles, I always knew there was so much more to be written about Africa. Throughout my dozen post-Africa years there's been a distant, haunting drumbeat in my head: write about Africa, write about Africa, write about Africa . . .

I think now, these years later, I understand that drumbeat more fully than when it first was heard.

Africa is so much like life. The continent's problems boggle the mind—economics in shambles, social revolutions, civil disorders, natural disasters, the ravages of hunger and illness, the daily struggle to survive.

Africa is the whole human experiment played out on a single continent. If Africa can make it, the human race, the entire planet can find a way.

Africa, like life, demands that we listen more and speak less.

Africa, like life, holds secrets not easily yielded.

Africa, like life, has abundant blessings to bestow upon the wise, the patient.

What has been said here of Africa could be said of most of the world's developing regions—which helps us make our point: such universal realities have a special meaning to people of the biblical faiths.

Such people know it instinctively: once you've been to Africa—or to wherever you've experienced humanity's oneness—you can never come all the way home.

Why? Because you don't have to. Because, though the place be distant and the language strange, you already *are* at home.

People who have been touched with the sufferings and joys of their brothers and sisters have many homes, whether they be in Africa, Alaska, Israel, Nicaragua, the not-yet-again land of Palestine, the USSR, the United States of America, or wherever.

It's nice to always be at home.

All the Young Men

It happens when I least expect it.

It may be while driving the freeway and glimpsing a highway crew at work; or perhaps at noon in downtown Little Rock on seeing crowds of young men leaving their office buildings; or when watching those television commercials filled with so many bright, young faces.

For a fleeting moment, such ordinary scenes seem strange to me, somehow out of place. What are all these stout young men doing here, anyway? Why aren't they where all healthy young men are supposed to be? Why aren't they—you know—in the Army, Navy, Air Force, Coast Guard, or Marines?

Then it strikes me: that kind of thinking is a 45-year-old flashback, a holdover that only those of World War II vintage can fully understand.

During the early and mid-1940s, when the United States was deep into the war in Europe and the Pacific and the military draft had all but swept our streets clean of strong young men, sights of groups of young male civilians were a rarity. Indeed, I suspect that among our most common collective memories of those days—along with Victory Gardens, eagerly awaited daily reports from overseas, ration coupons, shortages of certain foods and goods, and the dreaded prospect of a telegram arriving at the front door—are recollections of communities devoid of groups of stout young men.

Where had all the young men gone?

Gone to war, every one.

War, that ravager of nations, had gobbled up all our young men.

One would think that such a recollection would pass. Even though my own perception of the condition changed—I too was drafted, leaving yet one more empty place on our block—the potent image of village streets devoid of vigorous young men remains.

It's been that way, of course, throughout history. Whole generations of young men, in uncounted nations, have left home, many never to return. The thundering silence of their absence has left an unerasable emptiness across the earth.

In our current enlightened age we must now, of course, include women as fit candidates for what earlier generations called cannon fodder. We have thus advanced in the art of warfare. Women, too, may now play this game.

The point of these reflections?

The point is that in recent weeks there's been an encouraging glimmer among the ashes of humanity's too-often-dashed hopes for peace. Talk of a disarmament agreement among the superpowers and a proposal for peace in Central America are blowing on the coals of the world's heart, giving new life to the eternal dream of peace.

Perhaps it's too much to hope for—ominous rumblings still come from the Persian Gulf, Afghanistan, the Philippines, Central America, and elsewhere—but it's something.

To people of faith, such a "something" is significant.

Blow on the coals of the heart. Fan the ancient, fragile embers of peace.

Keep our young men and women where they belong—at home, free to live and let live.

Of Joy and Realism

Call me a cockeyed optimist.

Or a silly sentimentalist.

Or just a big pushover for media hype. Even a knee-jerk liberal—I don't care.

But whatever, call me hopeful, call me happy, call me joyful.

The cause of all this exuberance?

What else but the success of this week's Reagan-Gorbachev summit, at which it was agreed to abolish an entire class of nuclear weapons.

Although one's joy at such an achievement must be tempered by realism, the grandness of the event should not go uncelebrated. It is difficult to imagine a more appropriate Christmas gift and Hanukkah gift for the world . . .

Now, about that realism.

The agreement to abolish 2,611 intermediate-range nuclear missiles affects only about four percent of the world's nuclear arsenal—meaning that this world is still a very dangerous place. But as a symbol, the summit agreement is of grand significance, a monumental event—the first time the leaders of the world's two superpowers have proposed that an entire category of nuclear weapons be outlawed.

Though a lot of problems remain, concerning both nuclear and conventional weapons, the message is clear. The ancient arms race and the threat of annihilation by war—one of the ancient Four Horsemen of the Apocalypse—has been put on notice: the human race has had enough and isn't going to take any more!

That's a bold contention, yes. But what we witnessed this week at Washington is part of a long-emerging reality, a grand awakening that has been stirring for centuries. It is that the world's peace-loving people have risen up and demanded that their leaders give them a world safe from war.

The real heroes of the recent summit are all those people who, across the years, have voiced their opposition to the arms race and to the nuclear buildup.

A toast, then, to peace advocates throughout the world. Those persistent, hope-filled, dreamy-eyed individuals would not let us forget that human beings are made for more than cannon fodder.

Some more realism: "But can we trust the Soviets?"

Yet more realism: "But can the Soviets trust the Americans?"

That depends—on whether both groups prove worthy of trust. Given our own recent record in the Iran-contra affair, which dealt this country's credibility a severe blow worldwide, the answer depends on our own performance—as is true for the Soviets.

Perhaps one of the most remarkable aspects of this week's events at Washington was Soviet leader Mikhail S. Gorbachev's repeated theme: we are living in a time of new realities, a time that requires new ways of thinking, that requires bold measures. One could wish that challenge had come from our own president.

Let us savor the moment and rush to the next challenge. The hounds of heaven have caught the scent of a nuclear weapons-free world and they are hot on the trail.

Sic 'em!

I'd Rather Be Dancing

After two weeks of anger, frustration, and tension resulting from the current hostage episode, we suspect most Americans would sympathize with the bumper sticker proclaiming, "I'd rather be dancing."

Most of us would prefer doing anything—sailing, gardening, just plain working, or whatever—rather than being torn up inside by such crises.

But once again we're a nation in agony. Once again we're hobbled, seemingly helpless in the grip of terrorists who hold innocent people hostage for their lives. Once again the pain, the grief. Once again the edge of the precipice.

But aside from all other things such events do, they compel people of faith to search for answers, to re-examine the causes of the world's turmoil, to seek ways to peace, to always be the reconcilers, the peacemakers.

Perhaps we should understand when such happenings bring out the worst in us. Perhaps we shouldn't understand.

But whatever, such events do bring out our worst.

An example. A church member, asked by a television reporter her reaction on hearing that several fellow church members were among the hostages, exclaimed, "I think they should line all of them [the Shiite hijackers] up against the wall and shoot them!"

Even if such heat-of-the-moment reactions may be understood, they are, to our shame, echoed by many Americans, including, it appears, a few church members.

On the other hand, comments by some of the hostages themselves and their loved ones have been more temperate. Significantly, it seems to be a temperateness motivated not only by a desire not to make things worse but a sincere wish to understand the complex events that provoke such acts of terror. These comments seem to be acknowledging that such acts, however repugnant, are the bitter fruits of almost four decades of continuous warfare, disruption, and turmoil.

Let it be clear: terrorism is a crime, whether done by Shiite extremists in Lebanon or the United States-supported contras in Nicaragua.

Let this also be clear: so long as oppressed people do not have legal redress for what they perceive as denial of their due rights, there will be turmoil and terror in the world—whether by Shiites or Palestinians or Israelis or Sikhs or Nicaraguans or, to personalize the point, by citizens of the Confederate States of America or by our forefathers who fought in the American Revolution.

Peace, of course, is an idealistic vision, a dream. But it's a vision which all people of good will must join together to achieve. Only then may the whole world find reason to dance.

Let Us Speak of Life

Let us speak today of life.

Let us speak of dreams and visions and aspirations and goals.

Let us speak of the glory of our common humanity.

Let us speak today of joy.

If it seems insensitive, somehow impertinent, to speak of life and joy at the end of a week that has known such grief and sadness over the loss of seven lives in the explosion of the space shuttle *Challenger*, we suggest that the contrary can be true.

There is a time to grieve. There is a time to take up life again.

The latter time has come.

In retrospect, the national outpouring of shock and grief over Tuesday's tragic event is a remarkable thing both to experience and to behold. Although we contemporary beings are no strangers to violent death and although the spectacle of sending our young men and women into space seems now, after some 25 years, almost ordinary, there were unordinary and dramatic dimensions to Tuesday's event.

We had become excited with the prospect of a "common civilian," most appropriately a teacher, traveling to space to share its glories and mysteries with young students throughout the land.

To a smaller though no less significant degree we had shared the excitement of the shuttle's crew, each with a life story as vibrant as that of the young teacher.

It is no dishonor to those six astronauts that the focus of national attention has been on teacher Christa McAuliffe, for in a sense all seven were teachers and learners. All were students of life's grand mystery.

So where is the joy?

It is there, though the word may seem grossly inappropriate.

Joy, deep and quiet like a mighty river, is discovered in that powerful sense of bonding we humans feel most keenly in times of shared grief.

Joy, though subdued, dignified, and strong, is found in the rededication to life—to visions of human betterment—that follows in the wake of such events.

Joy, though heavy and often threatening, comes in the realization that we somehow have a stake in the death (as well as in the life) of every person—whether it be the sudden, dramatic death of an astronaut, the slow and sensational death by starvation of a child in Ethiopia or Detroit, or the violent death of an innocent villager in Afghanistan or Nicaragua.

We need not send to know for whom the bell tolls. We are bound together in the bundle of life.

Though frequently bittersweet, there is an abiding joy—and a great hope—in that discovery.

On Loving the Bomb

It was reported this week that a Delaware school board has ordered a seventh-grade teacher to stop teaching a course on nuclear war because the course was too "one-sided."

The teacher, William H. Hutchinson Jr., acknowledged that the material was "most definitely a one-sided [antiwar] approach," but said he was not given a chance to present "the other side of the issue" before ordered to discontinue the class.

The report raises an intriguing question: what, indeed, *is* "the other side of the issue" regarding nuclear war? In this age when nuclear weapons have the capacity to annihilate civilization and poison this planet for centuries to come, can there really be "two sides" to the nuclear war issue?

The question is timely because some current thinking suggests that a nuclear war is "winnable."

In a "special section" report October 17, the *Boston Globe* said: "In the 1980 campaign and since, Reagan team members have talked, at times almost casually, of nuclear war as thinkable, limitable, survivable and winnable; a corollary being that as many as 20 million Americans casualties would be acceptable."

Such thinking, as well as the complexity of the issue, has caused many Americans simply to turn the whole matter off, preferring to pretend the frightening prospect doesn't exist.

Edward P. Morgan, the social critic, has a word for such a reaction: "We are approaching Armageddon with less excitement than we manifest on the Super Bowl."

What, then, about "the other side" of the nuclear war issue?

It's difficult to refrain from offering a few points in favor of an all-out nuclear war. Consider the following thoughts on nuclear war:

■It would solve the post office's dilemma, as examined in a recent congressional hearing, concerning "plans for delivering the mail after a nuclear war." (*Poof!*—no more problem.)

■It would resolve a problem reportedly suggested by a kindergarten principal in a note to parents: "In case of a nuclear attack, the school buses will not run. Parents will be expected to pick up [!] their own children." (No comment required. The image is sufficient.)

■It would solve both our burgeoning Social Security and child day-care problems. (Neither old people nor children live very long after nuclear attacks.)

■We wouldn't have that pesky Equal Rights Amendment to push us around anymore. (The bomb is the great equalizer.)

■We wouldn't have to spend hundreds of thousands of tax dollars to decide whether to merge the Little Rock, North Little Rock, and Pulaski County school districts. (The bomb would accomplish that automatically.)

And so on.

A point is sought: that in spite of what some highly placed people are saying, the peacemakers are the most sane people around these days. They insist that we not forget that war, in this kind of world, is simply an unthinkable option. Such people are the true patriots of our time.

As for President Reagan's repeated comment that Americans in the peace movement, though "well intentioned," have been "influenced by persons from other countries," we acknowledge that he is correct. We herewith boldly reveal, for the world to see, the names of some of those persons from other countries:

Jesus Christ, Moses, the Apostle Paul, the Psalmist David, Mohandas Gandhi, Pope John Paul II, and Mother Teresa, to name but a few.

"Two sides" to the nuclear war issue? Only if we want humanity to commit suicide.

Home-bound Reflections

EN ROUTE FROM MANAGUA, NICARAGUA, TO MIAMI—Someone has just reported that the land mass we see below is Cuba, adding the comment—which may or may not be true—that we couldn't be here if we were flying in a United States airline rather than a Nicaraguan one.

In any event, the thought gives rise to a theme that has been present, although subliminally, throughout the last nine days as I have traveled in Honduras and Nicaragua with a nine-member group of reporters from the United States: that although human beings have

47

made fantastic technological advances during the past decades—accomplishments that have done so much to bring this world together—there are still vast chasms that separate us.

The theme, although it has such definite and threatening political and military expressions these days, is essentially a spiritual one. General Douglas MacArthur made the observation when signing the peace treaty with Japan following World War II: the world's problems are ultimately spiritual in nature, not military or political.

If such a contention is true, it has tremendous implications regarding what responses we make to "the problems" in Latin America—and, indeed, to all those vast, complex issues that threaten world peace today.

Such thoughts are too much, however, for home-bound reflections.

What crowds the mind now are more personal and immediate images and reflections:

■I see the face of a little girl in a poor barrio in Tegucigalpa, Honduras, as she watches our American translator, an attractive young woman who, to this poor slum-bound child, must symbolize an unattainable world of freedom, plenty, and security. The world's dreams are in that little girl's eyes.

■I see the impassioned faces of people with totally opposing causes—from one of the top leaders of the United States-supported "contras," who met with us behind closed doors in Honduras, to, ten hours later, the animated countenance of Nicaragua's Comandante Tomas Borge, bristling when he spoke of his mortal enemy.

■I see the stoic countenance of a young Sandanista soldier, one of six teenaged veterans of border skirmishes who, with their AK-47 rifles, provided security while we rode in an East German army truck during an unforgettable twelve-hour trip to the border combat zone.

■I see the zealous faces of American nuns and other

United States citizens who have devoted their lives
—and who risk them daily—in ministry to Nicaragua's
poor. I still feel their pained exasperation at what they
perceive as the cynicism of the press and of other
Americans who insist on imposing their own patterns
and measurements on Third World issues.
In a few minutes our plane will land in Miami. It's
such a small and beautiful world, really. There's got to
be a way to hold it together.

Of Drums, Gunshots, and Children

The big drums are best. You can literally feel their marvelous rumblings as the concussion reverberates through your body and ricochets between the tall buildings in downtown Little Rock.

It's Tuesday, October 6, and it's Arkansas State Fair
Rodeo parade time again.

It's also the morning on which Egypt's President
Anwar Sadat has been shot. At this time, as the parade
reaches downtown Little Rock, many early arrivers
don't know about the shooting and there's still no certain word whether the Egyptian leader is dead or alive.

Too, there's a tantalizing uncertainty about what this
latest madness could mean to the delicate balance between peace and war in one of the world's most volatile
regions.

*The bands are coming now, high school bands from small
and larger towns throughout the state. Young people marching, intent on their music, sharing the enthusiasm of the occasion. It's a parade! And from the preview, overhead from several blocks away, there'll be plenty of drums to enjoy.*

How much more tension do we have to endure? How
many more assassinations do we have to experience?

49

How many more *can* we experience?

People have always been killing people, of course. But, as only the hackneyed phrase can express it, terrorism has become a way of life. Perhaps that is why the drums seem so right today. Only drums are adequate for feelings like these.

There's something universally appealing about a parade. One should never miss a parade. Even if it happens to be when a world leader has been shot. *Especially* when a world leader has been shot. One needs parades. Particularly on days like this, one needs parades.

Too, one needs drums at a time like this. In addition to whatever grand things drums do for the digestion, vibrating one's insides the way they do, they're bound to do other, more remarkable things for the spirit.

Drums do inexpressible things for the soul. Perhaps if they could be just a little louder, a bit more whatever it is that they are, they could break through to some deep, vast mystery-place where the heart hides its secrets and nourishes its most cherished miracles.

Drums do it best. At least today.

Little children, held high on daddy's shoulders, don't know about a world gone mad with terrorism. Nor should they. They have their own gifts to bring to the rest of us, and those gifts are of such greater value than so much of what we are giving them.

We should watch little children at parades, and, as with drums, we should listen to them.

The high school band passes, majorettes and flag-bearers and musicians all joining in a rousing, robust celebration of life. There's something so poignantly beautiful about it all on this glorious fall afternoon, even though perceived hazily through stubbornly irrepressible tears.

Soon the next band will be along. Maybe it'll have drums, too.

Just Too Busy

It occurred to us late the other afternoon, long after this column was supposed to have been written, that we might say to the folks on the other side of this tiny cubicle (wherein our whole religion staff is kept from the public) that we're just too busy to write a column this week.

But on reflection we changed our mind. That could give them ideas.

So, after rejecting such possible topics as the mass-baptism potential of Little Rock's new slackwater harbor or the relationship of quantum physics to neo-orthodox radical conservatism, we awaited further inspiration.

It was soon to come: John, why don't you tell them about your vacation!

A splendid suggestion.

What we did last week on our vacation was to walk three hundred miles throughout the whole of all New York City; ride for six weeks on the Big Apple's lovely subway system; see four million museums, eight jillion tall buildings and fourteen thousand relatives and near-relatives; and then sit four days on our airplane while waiting for mechanics to repair something we could have fixed in twenty minutes. Maybe ten minutes.

But, as they say, that's what vacations are for—to get your mind off whatever it is you do all the rest of the time. Well, it works. Not once last week did we think about not writing a column this week.

The whole business makes one think of all those things that human beings don't want to do but ought to do and need to do and are supposed to do.

Like, for instance, telling loved ones we love them. And doing things that heal old wounds. And saying things like "I forgive you" and "Please forgive me" and "I don't want to do that anymore" and "Don't you think we can work this out?"

There are other things we human beings ought to get around to. Like making peace rather than war. And cleaning up this scarred, once-lovely planet, so fouled by our poisons and pollutions and torn apart by our animosities and greeds.

And, too, it wouldn't hurt us to not be so busy all the time that we can't right those ancient wrongs that keep brothers and sisters apart, that keep people in bondage, that breed violence and terrorism.

And perhaps if we weren't so busy with important things, we could find ways to overcome all those influences that threaten life for the precious children of this land, that drive teen-agers to suicide and parents to despair.

It seems there are a few things yet to be done. But we're pretty busy at the moment. Maybe later.

Avocations

Because It's There

Why do they do it? Why would anybody in his right mind want to ride 100 miles on a bicycle in one day? And on a Sunday, at that, when a lot of truly fun things could be done instead.

There are a lot of reasons, really. And most of them, while they make perfect sense to the seasoned rider, still sound unconvincing to the uninitiated.

They do it because it's there—the highway. They wonder what's around the next bend and over the next hill and beyond the range of mountains in the distance.

They do it because you can't ride a bicycle indoors. They do it to worship the sun, to feel the wind in their faces, to smell the fresh-mown hay, the bitterweed, the marshy land. They do it to see the little farms where life goes on, and the abandoned ones, with watercolor barns soon to go the way of all things.

They do it to see the land, to remember what is too casually taken for granted: the miracle of it all. Whether it's on Arkansas's vast Grand Prairie, as was Sunday's Century Ride, or a cross-continent tour or a neighborhood meandering. They do it to survey the land and be thankful.

They do it to see horses standing still in the early morning mist. They do it to pass the little dairy barns, with their sweet, pungent aroma, even the pigsties and barnyards with their own strangely appealing odors.

They do it for the fun of being with another rider or riders. For the fellowship, some would call it. Camaraderie is a better word, but not quite adequate either.

They do it for the solitude. For, to many riders, bicycling is a solitary sport, providing a gardening-time for the soul, an incubator for the spirit.

But mostly, cyclists in such events as Sunday's

Century Ride do it to compete with themselves. They do it just to see if they *can*. Or to remind themselves that they are up to it. They do it to feel the tightness in the muscles; even, yes, to feel the soreness the next day.

And, perhaps most fundamental of all, cyclists—as do all sports enthusiasts—compete in response to some primeval call, some ancient demand to do the difficult, to meet a challenge, to accept a dare from the impossible.

They do it to feel good, even though at times it feels bad.

And, be they young or old, they do it to store the experience in their memories. Though always planning on the next long ride, they know that if it should be the last, they'll have it, and all the others, to savor when winter, not to be denied, fulfills its own haunting promises.

Fort Smith to Little Rock: Some Kinda Bicycling

Before the onward march of the famous explorer, a path opens through the thickest jungle; broad rivers shrink to rivulets; the rugged pass becomes a smooth highway; wild animals flee in dismay: the American axe hews down sturdy forest; the frail canoe descends foaming rapids and crosses inland seas and the Dark Continent gives up the secrets that have baffled the world for thousands of years.
       —*Explorations and Adventures of Henry M. Stanley,*
       H. Davenport Northrop, D.D., 1889

Man, that was some kinda tough bicycle ride!
       —*Journal,*
       John S. Workman, A.B., D.D., October 1982

Okay, let's get this over with right at the top.

Yes, it could be called silly or dumb or stupid, or at least unbecoming, for a 55-year-old man who is supposed to be dignified—the religion editor of a newspaper—to ride his bicycle from Fort Smith to Little Rock.

Yes—to ride his bicycle from Fort Smith to Little Rock.

But, on the other hand, it doesn't have to be any of those things. (Everybody's got to be somewhere.) It could have been just a fun thing to do, an adventure, the kind of joy that shouldn't be granted only to little boys and girls.

What it was was a dandy bicycle trip, the kind that children of all ages dream of:

A three-day, 175-mile journey, lazily enjoying the beauties of the countryside. The adventure was idyllic—three grand fall days, perhaps the last of their kind of the season, the open road, the magic of a campfire at night, the aroma of food cooking on a wood fire, the warmth of a sleeping bag, and the sound of coyotes howling in the moonlight.

But a bicycle? What on earth could possess a supposedly reasonably intelligent man to ride a bicycle halfway across the state of Arkansas?

Several things.

For one, mountain climbing in the Andes is out of the question this time of the year. A trip through Tibet really isn't practical at the moment. Bicycling across China will have to wait a year or two. And sailing to the South Pacific is just too much to swing this year.

So, it has to be Fort Smith to Little Rock on a bicycle. One must make compromises these days.

Some would contend that such escapades, real or imagined, are an escape. Perhaps it is so. But they are an escape to something, rather than from something. They are an escape to some grander realities, a retreat from the confines of an office building, city noises, the pressure of deadlines.

Such adventures are flights toward life, not from it.

They are pursuits of holy grails.

"[Stanley] received one of the most important and difficult commissions ever given to mortal man. . . . Difficulties that would have appalled other men at the outset were as nothing to him; obstacles were cast aside as by faith that moves mountains into the sea. Threatening dangers did not turn him from his lofty purpose. On he went, across plains, down through valleys, through tangled jungles, over almost impassable rivers, displaying everywhere and always the most wonderful heroism and endurance, until the world was startled at his discovery and will evermore applaud his magnificent achievements. . . . Henry M. Stanley is one of the great heroes of modern times."

Entering the outskirts of Bloomer (Sebastian County) now, on state Highway 22. The little handlebar-mounted radio gives forth with the Sons of the Pioneers—who else?—doing that old classic, "Cool Clear Water." One muses, while watching a tumbleweed being blown across the deserted highway by the hot autumn-sun-inspired breeze, that they don't make songs like that anymore. Nope.

This particular trip, long in the planning, was supposed to have been made with our youngest son, before he left for college. But schedules didn't allow that and attempts to recruit colleagues in the office were of no avail. So, once again, the sturdy explorer is destined to face the wilderness alone.

The trip, 174.2 miles all told, followed Highway 22 from Van Buren to Dardanelle, Highway 7 to Centerville, Highway 154 to Oppelo, Highway 9 to Paron and Kanis Road into Little Rock.

Overnight stops (sleeping in a lightweight two-man tent) were made at Shoal Bay on Lake Dardanelle (two miles north of New Blaine on Highway 197) and Petit Jean State Park.

The bicycle was packed with two pannier bags (containing clothes and cooking gear) and a sleeping bag on the rear carrier and, on the front, a handlebar bag (with food, camera, windbreaker, and stuff) with the rolled-up tent slung underneath. A camp chair (all the comforts of home) fit neatly on the frame, just above the pedal crank.

Total weight of gear, 38 pounds. There is something philosophical—is that the word?—about bicycle camping (as with backpacking, also). You've got all your gear together, you're independent, you're facing a challenge, there are uncertainties and risks ahead—perhaps even dangers—and the open road is before you.

Granted, that could get old after a while, but for a time it does something for the soul. Perhaps many of our troubles as a modern technological society can be laid to the fact that we've lost touch with such elemental realities.

A grand moment: hearing, while camped at night, both at Shoal Bay and Petit Jean Mountain, coyotes howl in the moonlight. I'd forgotten that this happens in Arkansas. Though I'm sure that this, too, would get old if you had to listen to it every night, it adds a remarkably delightful dimension to a solo camping trip.

One coyote, who begins the long high-pitched wail, is quickly joined by another and then another until it seems the whole woods are filled with howling wild animals.

Coyote listening while solo camping is enhanced if it happens while you're reading in your tent, by candlelight, the book you've brought along: *Forbidden Journey* (what else?), the account of a six-month caravan trip across China in 1935 from Peking to Kashmir, by Peter Flemming, a correspondent for the London *Times,* and Kini Maillar, a Swiss journalist and adventurer. They faced fierce Tibetan wolves or, even, perhaps one of the dreaded Gobi whatyoumacallits. Fun.

A state Game and Fish Commission official later told me that Arkansas coyotes "howl that way to communicate with each other." They sure communicated with me.

"The hardy life that [Stanley] led developed his physical strength and made him a man of nerve and iron. His power of endurance already showed itself. Few could travel farther or endure more fatigue than he. If any enterprise was planned that required a brave spirit, Stanley was the young man who was found equal to the occasion. He was a brave, strong character, just the one to cross seas, climb mountains, wade rivers, endure hardships, explore continents, . . . [He] was not in the habit of turning back from the face of danger. . . . It was not in the nature of things that so bright and spirited a young man should long remain idle."

Coasting into Paris now, my bicycle flag fluttering and snapping a dandy staccato.

Nice of those public school officials to let classes out and arrange for all the elementary children to line the streets, for blocks, waving little Arkansas flags and cheering my arrival as the high school band plays the theme from "Chariots of Fire"! A stirring moment indeed.

(Just kidding. Nice thought, though.)

Back in the office, a colleague puts the question: What does one think about while pedaling a bicycle all day long?

Good question. A bit silly, but good.

I can't remember.

Most all trips afford some highlights, moments to remember, as it were. This one was no exception.

■ . . . Moving along great, about noon on the first day out. Liz will be along any minute now, driving back to Little Rock from our son and daughter-in-law's home into Van Buren. She's following the first part of my route this first day to check on me, to see if all's well. It'll be great to see her, to impress her with how far I've come.

He came over the top of the hill, meeting me, the state trooper did. Immediately he swerved to the side of the road, motioning me to pull over.

"Got a message for you," he shouted through the opened patrol car window. "Call your home."

I had to double back a couple of miles into Caulksville

60

to get to a phone, wondering all the way what kind of emergency message awaited me.

It was Liz, in Van Buren: "John, I can't find the car keys."

Of course she couldn't—they were right here in my pocket . . .

She got the opportunity to borrow our son's car, bring our four-and-a-half-year-old grandson with her, and make the lovely 70-mile drive to pick up the keys, which I left for her at a gasoline station in Caulksville, assuring her not to worry about me, that I'd be all right. Funny how wives forget to ask about car keys.

■. . . That's about the third time I've seen that same car—going back and forth along this highway, he is. Must be some crazy fellow who's lost. Poor man.

I was coming into the Shoal Bay camp area when I first heard it—strange noises coming from the woods. Some silly folks have lost their dog, I figured.

The sound persisted and then, with great laughter, out of the woods came two familiar figures: the *Gazette*'s own Arkansas Traveler and his wife, Charlie and Judy Allbright. What a small world! After a brief visit, during which well-wishing and an offering of delicious cake were left with the stalwart bicycle adventurer, they went on their way, hunting for other funny things to write about.

■. . . The hot shower at Petit Jean State Park and the trusting generosity of the good folks at Ezell's Cafe in Perryville, where, when I had only 83 cents left, they sold me, on credit, one of the world's all-time best meals.

■. . . Moving along Kanis Road, on the third and final day, I spot a roughly painted yard sign proclaiming, "Apple For Sale." I was hot and tired and the thought was tantalizing, but I figured they'd already sold it.

■Numerous landscapes, etched in life's golden book of memories, as they say, will remain: brilliant blue skies, the clean, clear atmosphere of splendid fall days, the grandeur of maple and gum trees changing color, the rustle of dried soybean leaves in the field, their dull chartreuse and rusty gold offering a horn-of-plenty banquet for the eyes and soul. Moments of a lifetime.

Mileage covered: first day 66, second day 40, third day 68. No flat tires and no mechanical trouble. Not a bad performance for my $25 bicycle, I'd say. A piece of cake all the way.

Toughest part of the trip: pedaling nonstop up the west end of Petit Jean Mountain. Easiest part: eating.

"It must be evident by this time to the reader that Stanley was at home everywhere. He did not stop to consider climate, country, language or hardships when he was to undertake one of his daring enterprises. . . .

"After untold privations, daring deeds and amazing triumphs, Stanley emerges from the wilds of the Dark Continent amidst the acclamations of both hemispheres. The nineteenth century records no triumph more sublime. . . ."

Two neighbors and a guy in my Sunday school class said they thought my trip was really something.

On the Third Day

It's the middle of the afternoon on the third day and I'm huffin' and puffin' halfway up one of the toughest, although most beautiful, bicycle climbs in Arkansas: Rich Mountain, in Polk County. My destination, after leaving Little Rock two days ago, is Queen Wilhelmina State Park, five miles from the Oklahoma state line.

The disc jockey at the Mena radio station has just volunteered, via my little handlebar set, to help his listeners make it through the afternoon. To prove it, he's just given us Willie Nelson wailing "Take It to the Limit One More Time."

Stay with us, Willie. Ole Jim—my bicycle—and I are

almost there. It's been a grand trip.

Bicycle camping in Arkansas in the fall is hard to beat—clear blue skies, warm days, marvelous vistas from mountaintops and valleys and cool—even crisp—evenings by a campfire. Add good food and a warm sleeping bag to help you make it through the night and you know what good camping is. And, if that's not enough, there's the sound of coyotes howling in the distance to lull you to sleep.

The only thing missing on this trip is good companionship on the road. Once again my compatriots have deserted me, and I'm destined to go the distance alone. Where are today's hardy souls?

This trip was planned with a couple of deliberate objectives: to travel highways I've never been on before, and to try a limited distance on gravel roads, just to see if it is practical to travel Arkansas's backroads on a ten-speed bicycle.

The outcome, in both instances, was a happy one. As for traveling unknown roads, when one isn't aware of what's ahead, what's around the next bend in the highway and over the next hill, the journey is more interesting. Kipling writes of the attraction: "Something lost beyond the mountains. Go and find it."

As for travel on gravel—a definite no-no for most bicyclists—it proved to be an exciting and gratifying experience, although not without its liabilities.

My route, designed to include about 20 miles of gravel road, took me from my home in west Little Rock west on Markham Parkway, through Ferndale to Paron, north on Highway 9 about three miles to Brown's Corner, then west through the Winona Wildlife Management Area to Highway 7 (the 20-mile gravel stretch).

Then south on Highway 7 to Jesseville, west on Highway 298 to Story, south on Highway 27 to Washita, and west on Highway 88 to Mena and, finally, the twelve-mile climb to Queen Wilhelmina State Park.

Total distance: 156.6 miles. Miles traveled daily: first

day, 39.7 (shorter because I was unable to leave Little Rock until noon); second day, 55.7, third day, 61.2.

My gear, packed in two panniers on the rear carrier and one handlebar bag on front, with a lightweight two-man tent slung underneath, weighed 40 pounds. In addition to the regular camping gear—sleeping bag, air mattress, two changes of clothes—I carried food for two meals and extra water, since I was unsure of water and food sources through the Winona Wildlife Management Area, and points west, for that matter.

The extra water, in a gallon "freeze pack," proved a real necessity. That, plus one regular and one oversized bicycle water bottle, met my daily drinking and sponge bath needs.

The stretch of gravel road was of interest from several standpoints: solitude—I met only two vehicles during the first day and three the second (the latter being large logging trucks, which raised billows of fine, choking dust)—and the beauties and delights of back-country travel.

Indeed, in sections where the forest has been clearcut, one could imagine he was traveling on the Alaska Highway or in the Australian outback.

After cycling on more than 20 miles of gravel—about half that distance on roads that had just been graded—my assessment is that such a distance on gravel is the equivalent, in time and energy, of about 60 miles on hard-surface highways. But when you consider the adventure factor, the gravel is well worth the effort.

Gravel travelers should take note, however, of the precautions required: attention to speed (slow is the word), alertness to large rocks in the road, extra care in descending hills, and continuous care in avoiding spills.

I carried two extra inner tubes and one tire, but had no flat—and, more importantly, no spills.

It should be noted my bike is not the lightweight model used by many cyclists today. It is the more traditional model—steel rims (with eight-year-old standard

27-by-1¼-inch tires) and a "stock" frame. Gravel travel on the popular lightweight ten-speeds with alloy rims would be another matter.

If care is taken, travel on gravel, with its access to some of the remote areas of Arkansas's beauty, is a rare treat indeed.

An example: late one evening, when rounding a bend, I came on a flock of seven wild turkeys. They appeared about as startled as I was, and after a brief pause to check me out, the larger bird, which I supposed was the mother hen, quickened her trot down the middle of the road and eventually took to the air, her retinue following, seeking an escape from this strange two-wheeler who had intruded upon their solitude.

However delightful bicycle travel on gravel may be, it is slow. By nightfall, I was only halfway through the 20-mile stretch, so I chose a desirable campsite a couple of hundred feet off the side of the road, where the dense forest bordered a large clear-cut expanse.

Because of the remoteness of the area and the extremely dry conditions and the lack of an abundance of water, I did not want to risk a campfire, so I cooked supper on my small campstove, a tin can fashioned to hold a Sterno can. Totally adequate—and safe.

One can hear interesting sounds when camping alone in the wilds. After drifting off to sleep to the accompaniment of coyotes wailing far to the south, I was suddenly awakened some hours later—my watch said 2:21 a.m.—by a loud crashing noise.

Elephants! Wild elephants stampeding!

On reflection, I figured that a large dead limb, high in one of the giant pine trees that, I guessed, rose to nearly 90 feet in height, had chosen this moment to "let go" and in the process took other limbs with it, crashing to earth about 100 yards from where I was camped. A formidable sound indeed.

If the experience accomplished nothing else, it settled once and for all that ancient question: if a tree falls

65

in the forest and no one is around, will there be a sound? There was nobody around for miles—and believe me, there was a sound!

Daybreak looks good after you survive the only known wild elephant stampede in Arkansas history.

Place names and roadside signs are among the numerous delights enjoyed by bicycle travelers. A few: "Mean Dog" (enough said for the cyclist), "Little Hope Baptist Church" (but, one would suppose, great faith); and such identifications as Rocky Creek, Fiddler Creek, Hackberry Creek, and, in one instance, a four-line sign declaring, "Oden Ball Field—Green Tree Project—No Alcohol—Have Fun."

At the close of the second day, half of which was spent completing the gravel stretch, Old Jim and I camped at Washita, on the east end of Lake Ouachita. Jim was so covered with dust, and the lake so inviting, that after unpacking him I led him into the water, being careful not to get his axles wet, and gave him a good bath, taking care to rotate the chain numerous times to clear away as much of the grit and grime as possible.

You might say Ole Jim got a veritable baptizing.

The next morning, with the chain dry, I applied a generous coating of WD-40.

According to plan, my wife, Liz, met me at Wilhelmina, where we camped on the last night of the three-day trip. The next morning we loaded Ole Jim on top of our car—a perch he seemed totally willing to occupy—and completed our one-week vacation with a couple of days' camping on Magazine Mountain.

To Conquer the Khyber

■*Fantastic! Incredible! If you can hang on for a couple of more minutes, John, you can make it . . . The first Arkansan to conquer the Khyber Pass by bicycle! Tremendous!*
■*The Kalahari Desert was never this dry, this deadly. It's tough, but you've got to do it, John. They're counting on you. There are women and children in that stranded camel caravan and you and your bicycle are their only hope. You've got to get to that next native village . . .*
■*The Great Wall of China by bicycle! Unbelievable! Ninety-three days through storms and darkness, bandits, brigands, and wild animals—and, worst of all, fleas in your sleeping bag! But worth it? Does a dog bark? Does a camel bite?*

Actually, it wasn't really the Khyber Pass. It was Thornburg Mountain in Perry County. Nor was it the Kalahari Desert. That was a stretch of Highway 9 between Paron and Williams Junction. The women and children idea? That came from a stalled car by the grocery store-gasoline station at Oppelo, near the east end of Petit Jean Mountain. And that Great Wall stuff, that was a winding, narrow bit of Kanis Road somewhere between Ferndale and the new Markham Parkway.

What it was was a bicycle trip. And when you're half-a-century-plus-four, fantasies are not only allowable, they're commendable. Even necessary.

As bicycle trips go these days—cross-continent journeys are not at all uncommon—this one was unspectacular: a two-day round trip adventure from Little Rock to Petit Jean Mountain. Distance traveled: 136.8 miles. Piece of cake, we veterans of the road call it. A pushover.

Bicycle trippers are required to do at least three things (it's a law somewhere): talk incessantly, to anyone who will or won't listen, about their most recent trip; keep a little journal about happenings along the way; and write something about it later.

I've done plenty of the first, enough of the second, and what you're reading now is evidence of the third.

■Saturday, June 27, 6:27 a.m., mile 0: late already! I was supposed to be off by 6:00 a.m. Dagnabbit! But when you have to go to a church dinner the night before your big trip (when you'd really rather be packing and getting things ready), there's a lot left to do in the morning. Like checking lists and making sure the bike is in order. (All that stuff, really, is part of the fun. Anticipation and planning are, indeed, an enjoyable part of the adventure.)

Got your four oranges? Camera and film? Two water bottles and Cub Scout knife? Flashlight? Change of socks, shorts, underwear, T-shirt—each packed in separate plastic produce sacks left over from purchases at Skaggs? Packed the pannier bags? (They look neat, hanging there on the back rack. Can't decide whether they resemble Pony Express saddlebags or motorcycle stuff. They'll probably be both at intervals along the way.)

■6:31 a.m., mile 0.4: less than one mile traveled and already I have to stop! Won't get far this way. Forgot to put my warm-ups on over my regular cycling outfit—shorts and T-shirt. The morning air is great but a bit chilly when moving. This feels better.

■6:39 a.m., mile 3: on Markham Parkway, heading west! Yahooo, finally under way for sure.

What's that ahead? A jogger in the distance, approaching through the morning mist. Forlorn-looking lad. Looks a bit like . . . Could it be? Yep—it's the *Gazette's* own Galloompher, doing his thing.

"Hey, Pauleee!"

"Hey, Johneee!"

"Let's go to Petit Jean!" (That'll get him.)

"Woooah!" (And a look of disbelief.)

Runners. Humph. Let's see him make 136.8 miles in

two days! Envy was all over his face . . .

Now to settle down for some serious pedaling. No hotdogging, just steady, easy going. The trick with ten-speed touring is to maintain a constant cadence. The pros recommend between 60 to 90 revolutions of the pedal-crank per minute. I find about 60 to 65 rpm best for me. Arkansas's hills keep the ten-speeder busy shifting through the full range of gears in order to maintain the proper cadence, but it's the secret of success—less fatigue, better mileage per hour.

There have been a bunch of bicycles in my life. A half-dozen or so, I suppose. Some were even new. Like the first one I can recall, on about my fifth Christmas. It was in the Methodist district parsonage at Fayetteville. Santa Claus, in an effort to conceal the bikes—there were two of them!—had hidden them in a closet. My brother and I, on a pre-Christmas searching expedition, came upon them. Our excitement was so great we couldn't conceal it from Santa's best friends, Mommy and Daddy.

Our parents, in a panic, said they were keeping the cycles for our neighbors. Our tears were so plentiful, our crying so painful, they had to "'fess up" and tell us that actually Santa had left the bikes for us. Seldom have tears been replaced so quickly by joy.

■8:10 a.m., mile 16: it's going great. Beautiful day! Warm enough now to take off the warm-ups. With the added 20 pounds in the panniers and front bag, the going's a bit slower than otherwise. No problem, though.

It's nice, having your stuff packed all neat and proper. A good, got-it-all-together, self-sufficient feeling.

What is it with bicycling, anyway? What's the big deal about bicycle tripping?

As with any activity or hobby, there's an appeal about bicycling that sometimes is difficult for the uninitiated to appreciate. There are elusive dimensions to the attraction.

There's challenge: can you really cover that many miles? There's uncertainty, even a mild element of risk: will your bike hold up? Can you handle any mechanical problems that might arise? Will the weather remain favorable?

Too, there is, for want of a better explanation, the "back-packer syndrome" associated with biking: you've got all your stuff together in a neat little pack—food, clothes, tools—and you are mobile; you can get from here to there. There's a freedom about it. New places to see, and at your own leisure. There's space to think and to be.

Also, biking in Arkansas puts you outdoors in the midst of some of the most beautiful scenery available. There's the excitement of new vistas around the next bend. There's the delicious challenge of pumping up steep hills and tall mountains—and the exhilaration of plummeting down their "better" side. And there's the delight of long, sustained level stretches where, in tenth gear, one can clock off the miles at between 20 to 25 miles an hour, or even better!

Great feelings, all. Worthy of being stored in the memory for use on cold winter nights or in years to come when the rocking chair is about as far and fast as you can go.

Even parked in your storeroom, your bicycle is paying dividends. Your escape machine is there, ready when you are. And—the best thing about it—it also brings you home.

■9:10 a.m., mile 23: at Paron, about ten minutes behind my anticipated schedule. What the heck. A cold Pepsi tastes great. Buy four packs of M&M's—two plain, two peanut—for munching along the way.

The next major destination is Williams Junction, where Highways 9 and 10 meet. As with other legs of the journey—most divided into five- to ten-mile stretches—time is taken along the way to make photos or simply to stop and enjoy a particularly attractive mountain vista, of which there are many.

Highlights of the next stretch are Thornburgh Mountain—a devil on the ascent, an angel on the descent—and that oasis in the desert, Ezell's Cafe at Harris Brake.

It ought to be against the law to drive past Ezell's Cafe. Maybe even a federal offense. Twice on my journey I dined—the right word—at Ezell's. Twice I had meals worthy of grand acclaim. The first enabled me to pump up Petit Jean Mountain's steep east end (with a few rest stops along the way but, still, something I had been unable to do on a similar trip a couple of years ago when I hadn't eaten at Ezell's). The second Ezell's meal, breakfast the next day, provided the power to pump nonstop up Thornburg Mountain, Arkansas's Pike's Peak Jr. That should tell you something about the potential of one Ezell's egg with ham, biscuits, jelly, and coffee.

Ezell's will even feed people who travel by car.

What a trip that was! It was in the late 1930s and Jimmy and I—he was thirteen and I was eleven—had set out on what was to be the first in a series of Greatest Bicycle Trips of All Times. We rode from Fayetteville to Mount Magazine, a two-day journey of about 100 miles, spending the night in a boardinghouse at Paris. A couple of world travelers.

Among my many recollections of that adventure is oil in the peanut butter-and-jelly sandwiches—which constituted one of my first learn-by-doing experiences: never pack your lunch near the oil can.

We climbed the 2,900-foot Mount Magazine, then accessible only by gravel road, surviving a couple of dandy spills on hairpin turns.

Halfway up Petit Jean it comes to me: I'm not nearly the man I was at eleven.

■2:30 p.m., mile 62: the Visitors' Center on Petit Jean! Half of the mission accomplished! Take time out to call Liz and let her know all's well.

It's hard to camp out at Petit Jean Mountain. Twice I

have biked there, twice I have tried to camp out, and twice I have failed.

On the first trip, all the campsites were taken and there was no room in the inn (Mather Lodge). I called a friend over at Winrock International to see if I could pitch my sleeping bag in their barn. Certainly, he said. No problem.

The barn turned out to be plush air-conditioned guest quarters, complete with the thickest bath towels I've ever dried with, impressive sculptured soap imprinted with the Winrock monogram, and polished, delicious fruit in a bowl by the bed. Tough way to camp out.

That same experience was repeated this trip. My original plan was to travel with a cycling friend from Heifer Project International. But, being a Lutheran, he had a conflict and had to cancel—but only after having made arrangements with another friend at Winrock International for us to have overnight accommodations there.

The tough experience was relived: I had to spend the night in air-conditioned comfort, in a Winrock guest lodge with swimming, sauna, and recreation facilities offered. Too, I had to forego my planned Vienna sausage supper and, instead, eat a gourmet meal prepared by my good friend and host, Dr. Thanh Duc Nguyen, a livestock specialist with Winrock International and Heifer Project.

Thanh produced a masterpiece: pork chops prepared with a special Asian sauce, rice, pan-fried vegetables and, for dessert, a delicious flan with caramel sauce. And, thanks to the absence of my Lutheran friend, I, as principal guest of honor, was served two pork chops. Not a bad way to camp out, I'd say.

■Sunday, June 28, 5:00 a.m., mile 68.4: beautiful morning! Plenty of time to be off by 6:00 a.m. Breakfast Number One—two granola bars and one apple—after which pack up and be on the way. (Breakfast Number Two was to be a couple of hours later at Ezell's.)

Uh-oh. Flat tire! And on the back wheel, too. Oh, well, this, too, is part of the adventure. This is why bikers carry those little air pumps that attach to the bike. Good news: it's just a slow leak. The tube, without being patched, maintains 70 pounds pressure so we'll see how things go. (It turned out to be a leak on an older patch and required only four or five repumpings during the trip home. Nice development.)

It's fun having the radio along for occasional diversions. To date, I've heard Orval Faubus reminisce about the good old days, McDonald's Storytime, Doug Brandon selling furniture at Russellville, and, this morning, a passel of radio preachers, the current one telling me that Jesus is due back at any moment and I'd better be ready. Not bad advice, I suppose. If it should be today, it couldn't happen on a lovelier morning.

The gospel music is great, but as I plummet down the face of Petit Jean Mountain at what feels like 90 miles per hour, I would have selected another number than "There's a whole lot of people goin' home. Bye and bye the time'll not be long—in the twinkling of an eye we'll all be gone. There's a whole lot of people goin' home . . ." . . ."

■Sunday, 1:45 p.m., mile 125: the ride back has been great. I've had probably two of the best days of the year for cycling; temperature in the low 90's with low humidity. Wonderful.

It's the bitterweed, I think, that does it best—brings back childhood memories. The hot wind off that abandoned pasture brings fleeting visions of summers on Magazine Mountain. Marvelous.

It's interesting how all of one's senses come into play when cycling. The sound of the wind, aromas from gardens, even odors from cow lots and pigpens all have their strange appeal. And those buzzards, circling high above to the west there, have their own beauty. An unpleasant bird in some respects, but how marvelous in flight! Now catching the high thermals, now silhouetted against deep blue sky, now black against fluffy

73

white clouds, now glimpsed through the tops of tall pine trees. What wonderful things they do for the mind.

Lots of little bunny rabbits out today. How John Thomas and Jennifer would enjoy them. Wonder what the future holds for this generation of grandchildren? If only that stupid bomb will give them a chance . . .

■Sunday, 2:45 p.m., mile 138: about half a mile from home! Great feeling. Still going strong; could probably even make a couple of more miles, maybe even three.

Rolling into Montevideo now. Crowds lining the streets—must be thousands, maybe millions, shouting, waving American and Arkansas flags and, yes, calling the Hogs! Marvelous! From Nome to Montevideo by bicycle in three weeks and two days . . . Fantastic!

Time Takes a Holiday

Toad Suck Bridge, Highway 60, July 7, 1:43 p.m.—Huff, puff; huff, puff. Another 100 feet and it'll be downhill again for a spell. Whooopee!

We've just topped the crest of the new bridge over Toad Suck Lock and Dam on the Arkansas River and our rapid acceleration, with its cooling, fast-rushing wind, is welcome indeed. We're some seven hours and 48 miles into our bicycle journey from Little Rock to Conway and our destination is just a short six miles away. Hooray!

Toad Suck Bridge has been something of a special goal for us, sort of a pre-victory symbol, as we've mapped and imagined our route on this First Official *Arkansas Methodist* Bicentennial Trans-County Bikathon which our seventh-grade son, Chuck, and I are making to honor our nation's and yours truly's birthdays, which both occur on the same day of the year. It's been a fun trip, not nearly as difficult as I would like to pretend.

There's no doubt about it, this Arkansas River Valley basin is the hottest spot we've encountered along our way. My little pocket radio, which I've taped to my bicycle bar, tells me it's 90 degrees at the moment in downtown Conway, and my slow pace up this long incline on the west side of the Toad Suck Bridge, hot sun reflecting off the bright, white concrete, confirms that report. But really, moving as we do on our trusty ten-speed bikes, the temperature isn't objectionable. It's been pleasant all the way.

Our passage along this "back way" to Conway has been a remarkable experience, a real joy. Our route follows little-travelled back roads, frequented only by those who call these parts home. To one accustomed to freeway travel, the scenery is other-worldly, reminiscent of childhood times. It's an inexpressible delight to move silently along these old and narrow asphalt lanes, past homey homes and small, neat family farms—it's almost like a journey back in time. We admire the gardens, smell the sweet corn and the hot, fresh-mown hay, are barked at by the dogs, marvel at the large sunflowers, and enjoy—yes—the odors of the pigpens.

We've just passed a little community revival tent, seating no more than 75, all prepared for the evening's service.

Here I am in the lead again—not too frequent a happening. (Chuck says I go faster downhill than he does because I weigh more. He uses another term which I don't appreciate.) I think, if I play it right, I can maintain this downhill racer speed and make that wide half-circle turn down below there and sail into that shaded picnic area in high form. I just hope I don't hit any loose gravel . . .

Aha! We made it! Now for a cooling drink from our water bottles.

Little Rock, 5:15 a.m.—Chuck has cooked our breakfast—ham and eggs—and has fussed at me for being so long in getting packed and ready to go. It'll be cool, traveling this early in the morning, so we put on long-sleeved shirts, and are to keep them on for several hours.

What a joy to be on our way! A beautiful day, the open road, and unknown adventures before us. Everybody ought to do this!

Pinnacle, 7:30 a.m.—Why do all the dogs chase and bark at me and not at Chucky? Don't they know that's why I brought him along on this venture? (Or did he bring me along for such a role?)

Natural Steps, 8:36 a.m.—Wheee! Whoever built this First Baptist Church couldn't have realized what a blessing it would be to a traveling Methodist preacher. It's rather unorthodox, I suppose, but "blessing" in this instance means lying flat on my back, on the church's front walk, with my feet propped up on the steps. And I suspect if the deacons knew how good it feels, they'd be right pleased, brother, to have helped a wandering sojourner in distress.

We stop at Martha's Cafe, a few minutes down the road in Roland, have chocolate milk and coffee, and exchange bicycle stories with the nice gentleman and gentlewoman behind the counter. He tells us of the big hill up ahead where, once, as he came down on his coaster bike, the chain came off, leaving him both "without and with"—without any brakes and with "a heap of thinkin' to do." She remarks that we "sure have a long way to go to get to Conway!" It pleases me to know that she, too, realizes this and I'm tempted to say something like "Oh, it's not much," but settle for complimenting her on the good cup of coffee.

Little Italy, 9:30—Somewhere in the Book it says something like "through much suffering you must enter the Kingdom." If that's so, I suspect I've just about arrived, for this hill we're climbing right now—it's about 100 miles long and 20 miles high— fulfills all the requirements. Anyway, it's solved one problem I've had—trying to think of a fitting biblical name for my bicycle. Now I've got it: "Much Suffering."

One mile west of Little Italy, 10:15—The hills are Italian—steep and beautiful—and so are the names on the mailboxes. And it's a far-away feeling I have at this, our sixth rest stop. I lie on my back in the grass, watch the sun and cloud patterns, misty through the oak trees, eat an orange and enjoy talk with my son. Forgotten are all those things going on in that other world out there that isn't nearly as real or as important at the moment as this one. Time takes a holiday and I become aware that here is another of those golden moments, to be etched in the memory, available for recall to give warmth to long winters in the years ahead . . .

We're soon on the way again. One nice thing about these back roads is that we can ride side-by-side for long stretches of time, without any traffic coming at us from ahead or showing up in our rear-view mirrors. It makes for nice conversation or sharing of music from our one radio.

Wye Mountain, 10:45—What a pleasant experience to become acquainted with "the daffodil lady" of Wye United Methodist Church, "Grandma Harmon," and enjoy good conversation with her. After a visit, we refill our water bottles and are on our way. Ahead is the best downhill run on the whole route, a two-mile grade down to Bigelow, where we'll hunt up some lunch. Hot dog!

Bigelow Mountain (downhill side), 11:20—Problems with my chain have put me a quarter of a mile behind, but with those solved and with this downhill grade and my modest 179 pounds working for me, I'll soon catch up with Chuck. I catch momentary glimpses of him way ahead, seeing his hunter's-orange bike flag flapping as he weaves around the "S" curves on this two-mile hill. At least I know he's still on the road.

Hot dog! What a thrill! I'll bet we're doing 150 miles per hour—at least!

Nearing Conway, 2:30—We're on the last leg of our journey now, and the anticipation of successfully completing our venture makes light work of these last few miles. We look forward to greeting parents and grandparents Big Jim and Big Sue, at whose home we'll spend the night before Mom picks us up in the car in the morning. If we could know about the cold watermelon awaiting us in Conway, we'd be there sooner than our 2:55 arrival, nine hours, five minutes, and 55 miles after leaving Little Rock this morning. It's been a good trip.

Little Rock, July 11—Like most good things, our long-planned-for journey is now history—over, it seems, too soon. But just as there is much joy in the planning of such ventures, there is also great joy in the remembering of them. So we now have three joys: the planning, the experiencing, the remembering.

But there is another factor, a haunting, elusive specter which must be confronted: an uneasy feeling of guilt in the presence of such joy. How can one justify enjoying life so much when there are so many who do not or cannot do the same? One feels that it is somehow impertinent to be so greedy for life and all it has to offer when there are so many who have so little of its joys.

And, too, as far as this publication is concerned, there is the matter of priorities. How to justify all this space when urgent issues of the moment, such as separation of Church and state, capital punishment, abortion, and terrorism and such, call for comment. . . ?

There are lessons buried deep in all of this, I suppose. But for the moment I choose to be excused from pursuing them. I elect, rather, to enjoy these recollections of hours spent with my son, moments when time took a holiday. Perhaps there is ministry even in this. Maybe especially in this.

Airborne: A Trilogy

1. Night Flight

Someday I must see that plane and know its pilot. They come over our home every night at about 11:20, headed west. I have it figured that it's a mail plane bound for Fort Smith.

But it's not just any mail plane. It has a personality, like in the old days of flying. I can tell that it's one of the older piston-driven types: it sounds like my car, as if it has a bad muffler or may not be hitting on all cylinders (though it's not an unsafe sound).

I like the sound. And you don't hear it from many airplanes these days. To hear it is a nostalgia-producing experience, akin to hearing the whistle of an old steam train. Wonderful!

As I listen to the plane overhead I can almost visualize the pilot. Sitting in an open cockpit, helmet and goggles (such as I used to have when I was six years old) securely fastened, white neck scarf flapping in the wind, his face is set heroically against the elements as he heads his craft into the unknown of the western sky . . .

That's one thing I like about my plane—it takes me on imaginary trips.

Another thing I like is that I know (if he really is going to Fort Smith) that in about 20 to 25 minutes from the time I hear him he'll be a thousand feet directly over our family cabin on Magazine Mountain on the Yell and Logan County line. I've heard him from there, too; and up there you can hear him coming from a much longer way to the east and can trace him almost until he lands some 50 or so miles to the west.

I find myself wondering about the pilot. Who is he? Does he have a family? Is he happy? Does he like his job? What does he think about life? How does he feel on ultimate issues? Does he think of the people over whom he flies, their joys and their sorrows? I think, really, that my thoughts of him are prayers; not spoken ones, but prayers nevertheless. For they plumb the mystery of persons, of adventure, of life and of meanings.

I shall most likely never see or know this pilot and his plane. But he enters my life for a few fleeting moments and is gone. Or are persons anyone, anywhere, ever really gone once they have peopled our consciousness? Could it be that once they have, we have a lasting "responsibility" for them?

I hope that he will fly well this evening. I hope that he will enjoy the beauty of this spring night.

2. Night Flight Caper

Scene: our office, Friday, May 3, 3:55 p.m. The telephone rings, our secretary buzzes:

"It's for you, Mr. Workman. Long-distance."

"Thank you."

"Hello?"

"Mr. Workman?"

"Yes?"

"Mr. Workman, this is Harold Zweiacher calling from Geary, Oklahoma."

"How are you, sir?"

"Fine. Mr. Workman, I have an article here from the *Arkansas Methodist* newspaper. It's called 'Night Flight,' about an airplane flying over your house in Little Rock . . ."

"Oh, yes!"

"Well, I think that I'm the pilot of that airplane . . ."

(Silence for a moment.) "You're kidding!"

No, he wasn't kidding. It *was* Harold Zweiacher and he *was* calling from Oklahoma and he *was* (and is) the pilot—one of two—who makes the flight which was the subject of the article. And how wonderful to hear from him!

After brief exclamations and greetings between us, he was eager to respond to some of the questions I had posed in the article. "I've got a list of answers down here for you if you want them," he said. And want them I did, so I answered, "Shoot." (We in aviation say "Shoot" a lot.)

Yes, it is a mail plane (one of a half-dozen or more which come in and out of Little Rock between 10:00 p.m. and 2:00 a.m. each night to all points of the compass). Yes, he likes his job. Yes, he has a family—his wife, one son, Troy, twelve, and a daughter, Dana, ten. Yes, he does think a lot about life, "just about like the average American, I guess." Yes, he does think about ultimate issues, and believes "everybody is concerned about what's happening in the world today." He's "not a fanatic on religion or anything like that," but does "read the Bible" and is "interested in Moses and those fellows." Yes, he does think about people and is "delighted to know that people down there are thinking about us," and "especially so in their prayers," he confides.

"How did you happen to see the article?" was one of my first questions to Harold. His answer opened up another interesting chain of coincidences. He told of how a young University of Arkansas student from Alabama, Harold Parker, III, also a pilot, had flown with him on occasion from Fayetteville. It was through him that the article had come to his attention. It seems that the student's mother in Alabama had sent the article to her son.

Wanting to follow up on this link in the chain of events, and since Harold Zweiacher did not know the Alabama Parker's full name or address, I searched our subscription files in the office and found a Mrs. Harold Parker with an Enterprise, Alabama, address. I sent off a "blind" letter, giving the reasons for my enquiry, in hopes that the party was "the right Mrs. Harold Parker."

The return letter said that indeed she was, and identified herself as "still considering Arkansas, and specifically Little Rock, as home," and that their church membership remains at First Church here, "which is how we happen to still receive the *Arkansas Methodist*."

She said she had seen the Night Flight article and had "let out a 'whoop!'" when she started to read it. "My husband asked what I was reading, and I said 'Listen to this—it may be about our Harold!'" She told of showing the article to her son and of his giving it to Harold Zweiacher. "The remainder of the chain of events you know more about than I do," she writes.

Of not unrelated interest is the way the Parkers' lives have been closely associated with aviation. Harold, II, is an instructor pilot at Fort Rucker, Alabama, the home of Army aviation, and Mrs. Parker has worked for the past five years for the U.S. Army Agency for Aviation Safety. Harold, III, a private pilot, is currently working toward his commercial certification. A younger son, Stephen, has a joint interest in creative writing and aviation.

Mrs. Parker writes that the type of plane (a Beech 18) used on the mail runs was the same type that the elder Mr. Parker had flown some years previously in Central America and the Caribbean and "was therefore always an interesting topic of discussion in our family."

And so it was through these circumstances, what I thought was such an interesting course of events, that the article came into the hands of my "night flight" friends.

On the evening after the call from Harold Zweiacher we were in touch again by telephone, arranging a visit and interview at the Little Rock airport. He told me of the other pilot on the run, Elliott "Cowboy" Martin, and I had a call from him on the next evening, arranging a similar visit.

The two fly for Pro Airlines, a charter service based in Rapid City, South Dakota, doing primarily mail charter service. Their route is between Little Rock, Oklahoma City, Fayetteville, and Fort Smith. One flies Monday,

Wednesday, and Friday, the other Tuesday and Thursday, and they alternate each week.

The plane arrives at the Little Rock airport at about 10:20 each evening, a busy time at the freight terminal. Several other mail planes, all twin-engine Beech 18s, (originally of late World War II vintage, though updated and improved) are in and out during the some 40 or so minutes our plane is being refueled and loaded with mail sacks.

During this time I visit with the pilot, each of us enjoying this unusual chain of events. I take a picture and the camera's flash brings another young pilot to the door, yelling to Harold, "What are you, a celebrity or somethin'?" Harold introduces me to Al Menzl from near Harrison, Arkansas, who flies for Stage Coach Airlines, another charter line doing primarily mail service. Harold explains what's going on, showing him the Night Flight article.

Al Menzl gets an obvious joy out of the whole situation and enters into it. He flies every other night to Kansas City and other points and tells of flashing his lights at riverboats and getting their signals back. "It really makes you feel good," he says, "to know that at least two human beings out there in the night are thinking about each other." He goes on: "We fly over these towns and think people down there are cussing us for all the noise. It really is good to know that people care."

3. Wild Blue Yonder

In visiting with Harold Zweiacher and Elliott Martin, our Night Flight mail pilot friends, about the possibility of my flying the U.S. mail with them, they suggested that the best arrangement would be for me to fly from Fayetteville to Little Rock, via Fort Smith. This, they explained, would keep me from having to go to Oklahoma, which I had always thought was a pretty pleasant experience. Anyway, since I had an upcoming date to be in Fayetteville, I knew that this plan could be easily worked out.

Having made contact with Elliott and reserving the co-pilot's seat (the only other seat on the plane since all other space is used for mail sacks), I took the commercial Skyways flight to Fayetteville and committed myself to fly home first-class air mail, special delivery, special handling.

I meet Elliott "Cowboy" Martin, a native Texan now living in Oklahoma, at the Fayetteville airport at about 7:30 p.m.—plenty of time to "pre-flight" our airplane before the van arrives to load the 1000 pounds of mail sacks. Elliott does his thing in preparing the Beech 18 and I do mine, which consists of "kickin' the casin's," about the only thing I can think of to do. I know that this doesn't look too professional, but it makes me feel better, anyway. It's a little ritual I always go through before tripping-out in the family auto. And besides, co-pilots have to do something too, you know.

Having been finally coaxed inside the airplane, I am strapped securely into my chair. I watch—and listen!—as the two huge Pratt & Whitney engines roar to a start. Elliott advises me to put on the radio earphones, both because of the motor noise and to enable me to keep check on what is happening with the three control towers that we will be in touch with: Fort Smith, Little Rock, and Memphis. "Roger" (cool!).

Elliott can't know, as we taxi out to the runway, the excitement of this experience for me. It was some 40 years ago at this same Drake Field, then only a dirt strip, that my brother Jim and I took our first airplane ride. We were strapped side-by-side in the open front cockpit of an old Travelaire biplane. How the wonder of that adventure came back to me now!

After getting clearance from the Fort Smith tower—assurance that we are free of all commercial aviation patterns for a 25-mile range—the big engines blast even louder than I had thought they would and we race down the runway and quickly rise above the familiar route of Highway 71. I glance out of the corner of my eye and note that Elliott is doing everything exactly right. I think of flashing him a "thumbs up" signal, as I imagine co-pilots always do after successful takeoffs, but I reconsider, thinking that this would be a bit too much. I consider saying something like "Well, it looks like the ole U.S. mail's gonna be on time tonight!" but dismiss this thought, too. I settle for easing back in the number two chair, trying to look relaxed, and straining to put an "Everything's A-OK" look on my face.

It's 8:55 now and the last of the summer evening sun lingers on giant cloud banks to the east, showing huge pink lambs trying to jump toward the deep blue above them. Beautiful! We continue to rise above the little mountain and valley farms and home sites. The earth is still warm enough to give off the buffeting-producing heat refections, and as we bounce around a bit I am grateful for the seat belt.

It becomes dark very soon and after leaving the closely-gathered lights behind us, the occasional night-watcher lights in the rural areas twinkle here and there. What a strange mixture of sights and sounds playing on my senses: the engine noise, the quiet pastoral scenes below, the radio chatter in the headphones, the mystery of all the dials, controls, and lights in front of me, and the dark Ozark range a few thousand feet below, hiding families and individuals with their joys and sorrows.

In what seems just a short while we can see the lights of Fort Smith some 40 or more miles in front of us. We listen as the tower gives landing and takeoff instructions to various planes, and soon hear the controller giving us the okay to land, indicating the proper runway. I feel the landing gear lower and lock in place. Our approach takes us across the entire width of the city and I enjoy looking down on it all, just a few hundred feet below us. I wonder how many folk down there are saying, as we do at our house, "There's our plane. He's on time tonight."

The runway lights come up to meet us and we are on the ground, soon loading more mail sacks. These sacks, totaling now I suppose about a ton of mail, are placed in the main cabin, which could accommodate about six or seven passengers if it were fitted with seats. The sacks are covered with a heavy net and strapped down to make them secure in flight. They are piled so high that Elliott literally has to crawl head-first over them to get back into the pilot's cockpit. ("He shouldn't have bothered," I'm thinking. "I can handle her from here on in to Little Rock . . .").

We are delayed at the end of the taxi-way for at least ten minutes while the tower lands several National Guard jets. Ten minutes of constant engine noise while not going anywhere, even with the eighteen cylinders idling, is something you can't ignore. It prompts Elliott to shout something about this being one reason pilots have hearing problems. I yell back, "WHAT?", and he smiles, realizing that he had forgotten for the moment that co-pilots have the same problem.

It is interesting to listen to the tower talk in the military jets, giving them clearance in turn to land. One reports not knowing if his landing gear is down and asks permission to "fly by" the tower to let them make a visual check. He is still some minutes away so we are given the okay to take off. I notice that the added half-ton of mail makes our gallop down the runway a bit more labored and also requires that I "pull up" a lot harder on the underneath side of my cockpit seat to get us into the air before we run out of runway. It is a good thing I do this—we make it. The Pony Express boys would have been proud of us!

Some five or so minutes later, when we are about over Booneville, we hear the tower talk with our jet pilot on the fly-by, reporting they can see that his landing gear is down and appears to be secure, giving him clearance to land. This experience, plus the almost constant exchange of communications between the several towers and many airplanes as we tune from channel to channel, impresses me with what pilots must take for granted: that even the ordinary elements of modern aviation are a wonder to behold.

The events form, too, something of a parable. For example: all during our flight we are "watched" by the radar scopes either at Fort Smith, Little Rock, or Memphis. How interesting and reassuring to hear the voices of those unknown tower controllers reporting that they "have us" at so-and-so location, giving us vital compass directions, altitude readings, and weather reports, guiding us all the way. We are in the hands of many unseen friends, and it is not only interesting, it is a good feeling, a parable with all kinds of sermonic suggestions.

Of particular interest to me is the fact that our course takes us right over Magazine Mountain and directly above our family cabin on the Logan and Yell County line. Although the massive mountain is dark—save for the two flashing lights on the antenna towers on its west end—we can see clearly the night-watcher lights of several farm homes whose locations I recognize and whose occupants I know. I think if these friends knew who is above them they'd say, "Why, that's Jim Workman's boy way up there actually flyin' the U.S. mails! Don't that beat all!"

We see the lights of Paris to the north, Havana just below us, then Belleville and Danville and later Ola. As Elliott points to Russellville far over to our left, I take off my headphones and yell to him that I have a son there in college. He replies, I think, that he has a sister living there, but the engine noise is so great I really don't understand him.

I am again surprised by how quickly we cover the ground. The air speed indicator in front of me has stayed on about 150 knots, about 170 miles per hour I believe, and the red flashing lights on KTHV's television tower on Shinall Mountain in Pulaski County are dead-ahead of us before I realize it.

I begin to recognize familiar landmarks below us. Over there are the K-Mart and Colony West shopping centers. Here on our right is the Baptist Medical Center. There is Presbyterian Village where my dear friend Flora Ashby makes her home, recovering now from a fall. Flora, among at least a dozen other west Little Rock residents, has told me that she listens now for her "night flight" airplane each evening.

I tell Elliott that we're just now above our house and he revs up the engines a bit, giving a roaring signal to my family below to let them know that their daredevil dad, the co-piloting roving editor, is back in town; their message to get the iced tea and Hershey bar ready.

There are many reflections one can make on such an experience. Certainly one is the pleasure of making these new friends and having the privilege of entering into their lives and the world of their professions. I now can visualize their experiences, their problems, their joys as they fly over each evening, coming in at about 10:20 and going out about 11:20.

Another reflection is to marvel at the unusual chain of events that unfolded in our acquaintance. And another, as I think of the many persons involved in the human services which are the daily responsibility of thousands of individuals, is the way we are really so dependent upon one another in our complex society. The mail pilots, the tower controllers, the Post Office workers—all are symbols of this interrelatedness of life.

And yet one other reflection comes in looking back on the original ponderings about our then-unknown Night Flight friends. The wonderings about them, who they were, how they felt about life, reflects, I submit, a need we human beings have to reach out to one another. We are never really complete until we can touch in meaningful ways the lives of those about us. Ships that pass in the night must always signal, for that is what living is all about. In this experience, my signals were received and returned in a most interesting and gratifying way.

And oh yes: Elliott, I heard you—but for sure!—when you came over our house that Friday evening after our Wednesday trip. You "roared" at just the right place, rattling our windows in a grand way! And Harold, I see you as you continue to come over with your landing lights on. I get your signals.

May both of you, and all travelers in the night, go with God's light upon your way.

Peace.

Vocations

Open Windows

Another reason I don't like air conditioning is because of all the sounds. (Not the air conditioner sounds —those are *noises*—but the good sounds, the outdoor sounds.)

With the AC on and the windows shut, I'm closed off from all those wonderful sounds from the out-of-doors, grand sounds that want to come into my room at night.

For a person who, in several previous incarnations, sailed the seven seas in an open boat and discovered unknown continents and climbed forbidden mountains and survived horrendous attacks by bandits in stifling desert heat and trekked across frozen wastes and rode a unicycle from Madrid to Peking and flew singlehanded around the world in an open-cockpit biplane and lived totally in the out-of-doors, closed windows in the summer are too much.

Windows are meant to be open, to let in the world-sounds and to afford easy access to the spirits of the night.

Who knows—perhaps all humanity's troubles have come upon us because we close our windows at night.

There's a theory: the world's salvation will come because there are people who refuse to close their windows during the summer.

Closed windows, if you didn't know it, breed bad spirits. Bad spirits, even evil ones, thrive in air-conditioned rooms, where the temperature is below 80 degrees. Show me a person who likes closed windows in summer and I'll show you a person inhabited by bad spirits.

Bad spirits need to get out of houses. How can they do that when all the windows are closed?

If God wanted windows to be closed, God wouldn't have made them openable.

Another thing: there are people who go through life

with their own personal "people windows" closed. If closed house windows are bad, closed people windows are worse. Much worse.

Not to be able to hear God, to catch God's sometimes faint whisper carried on gentle summer night breezes and in splatters of chilly storm-driven rain, is a tragedy indeed.

Not to be open to one's fellow human beings, to be shut off from other people, is a compounded tragedy. People windows are meant to be open.

If we must keep our house windows closed during the summer heat, we at least can open our people windows—to God and one another.

All together now: windows open!

Taking Comfort

Among those several things in which we take comfort is the report that Ernest Hemingway was something short of being the world's best speller.

Great for you, Ernie. We, to.

And that George Washington did, in fact, tell a fib or two while he was young—and maybe even several others after he grew up.

That's reassuring. At least we've never done that, by golly.

And that a noted theologian (whose identity we'll guard) didn't particularly enjoy going to church on Sunday evenings after being in the Lord's House all Sunday morning and half the afternoon.

Shame.

It's a funny thing about human beings. They take comfort in others' weaknesses. That's bad. It's not nice to make light of one's own shortcomings by calling attention to others' failures.

Far be it from us to do that sort of thing (though there are at least a couple of other writers in this building—maybe even four—who, as far as we're concerned, just don't. . . But we're certainly not going to get into that. No siree. Not us. Far be it from us to engage in cheap belittling.)

The Bible speaks to this sort of thing: "Rejoice not when thine enemy falleth, and let not thine heart be glad when he stumbleth" (Proverbs 23:17); "Rejoice with them that do rejoice and weep with them that weep" (Romans 12:15). In short, don't gloat over other folks' foibles, 'cause you've got plenty of foibles yourself, Buster.

But that kind of counsel is for sissies and certainly not for us contemporary might-makes-right types.

But do you suppose—do you just suppose—there's any possible application for the benevolent attitude in today's world? Or is this soft-on-your-brothers'-shortcomings business only for Sunday school and midweek Bible study?

Certainly the benevolent attitude won't work in today's tough, dog-eat-dog world where only the strong survive.

Come to think of it, maybe all that other stuff in the Bible—about love and forgiveness and reconciliation and all that—needs to be re-examined, too. Maybe all that's a lot of softhearted, muddleheaded, do-good kind of rhetoric that just won't work today.

But despair not. When faced with such tough ethical matters, we can always ask that question our leaders of contemporary American manners have inspired us to ask: what would Rambo do?

Do You Suppose?

Back at the chapel, some folks were praying.

They were prayers for Brother Charles, who was ill. Somebody remembered Sister Sue, who had just lost a brother after a long illness. One of the members said the group should remember the little neighbor boy who was to have surgery in the morning.

An old man, leaning on his cane, asked the group to pray for world peace.

Somebody mentioned that a couple, "having problems in the family," had asked for prayers. Someone else said the group should "remember the President and others in authority," those who bear heavy burdens of responsibility.

A woman, old in body but a child in mind, made her weekly request that the group "remember all our loved ones in distant places." And they did, as they had done every week for a half-century.

And so it went.

And so it goes, day in and day out, throughout this land and around this world.

Small groups—sometimes rather lifeless groups—at prayer.

Small groups, composed of folks who can be cantankerous at times, at prayer.

Small groups, sometimes containing folks who don't have very good track records at being good—folks who make mistakes, who have faults, who can be awfully unlovable at times—at prayer.

But still they meet, still they pray, still they keep on doing what religious people have done throughout the ages. (Do you suppose people pray because they can't *not* pray?)

We don't see much in the newspapers about such meetings. Such groups aren't flashy enough for television evangelists to make much over. And certainly such groups don't create enough trouble to attract the attention of newspaper reporters.

But still they meet. Still they go on doing what thoughtful people have done, in some manner or other, for centuries.

We'll probably never know whether such groups "really do any good."

We do know something, though. We do know that so far, something has kept this tired old world on course, even if precariously so.

Do you suppose that in this world where power really lies in bombs and political might and economic clout, that those small prayer groups, consisting of little, powerless people, could really have anything to do with keeping things going?

Do you just suppose?

On Spring Afternoons

Although the event is, I hope, some years down the pike, I sometimes find myself thinking about all those things I'd like to do when I retire. I've noticed of late that such thoughts come more frequently on spring afternoons—not unlike the very afternoon at hand even as I speak.

My list of retirement activities, though not yet on paper, is beginning to take shape in my head.

First, I'll get my pliers and straighten out that crooked edge on the spout of our family coffee pot. Spilling coffee regularly every morning of the year is forgivable if you've got to rush off to work, but it's not something you can put up with if you're retired.

Second, I'm going to patch that place on our garage

roof where the water drips into our storeroom and messes up the carpet on our floor.

Next comes retirement activity No. 3: straighten up my desk in my study. That task, naturally, will lead to retirement activity No. 4—building a tray or something for the top of my bureau so that all my important papers may be tended to within a month or so before being misplaced forever.

By the time I finish these several chores, it'll probably be about noon on the first day of retirement, so I'll have lots of time left to do whatever it is that retired people do—which is, I must confess, still something of a mystery to me in spite of having pondered the matter a bit.

And oh, yes. I'll need to fix the bird feeder on our patio so the sparrows won't scatter seeds all over the place. And while I'm at it, I can clean out the gutter along the patio roof, maybe even patch a spot or two where the water gushes out where it's not supposed to.

All this ought to pretty well take care of Day One of retirement. I can go to bed nicely worn out and be ready for Day Two.

Ah, retirement. I can hardly wait.

In the meantime, since retirement is a fistful of years or perhaps decades away, I might better spend my time on this lovely spring afternoon thinking about what I'll do with this year's vacation time.

Ah, vacation.

But hold on. This much leisure-time talk is about all I can enjoy. It's getting me down.

Perhaps those Bible-reading folks are right: happiness is discovered not so much in seeking one's own pleasure as in serving others.

If that sounds corny, that's okay. Think about it.

But don't think too long. Whatever your circumstances—employed or retired, young or old, rich or poor or whatever—there's something out there that needs to be done and perhaps, just maybe, you're the one to do it.

End of sermon. Congregation dismissed. Go thou and get with it.

Pickin' More Nits

A recent letter to this newspaper stated that our use of the words "gosh" and "golly" in this column constituted taking God's name in vain because such words are euphemisms for God. The letter writer acknowledged that some would call the criticism "nitpicking" and added, "If so, so be it."

Being something of a professional picker of nits, we defend our critic's right to pick. No nit is so small it should never be picked, we always say.

The observation brings to mind a dimension of the topic about which, in our opinion, there haven't been enough nits picked. That dimension: what does it really mean, as we are cautioned against in Exodus 20:7, to take God's name "in vain"? It must be something pretty serious, involving, we suspect, more than the use of words.

We suggest the admonition refers more to what "true religion" is all about—that it's a matter more of justice and love and forgiveness and reconciliation than of any "magic" related to the invocation of the names of ancient deities. We suspect the passage is saying one should avoid the peril of living one's religion "in vain"—that is, as ineffective, futile, and of no real value—and that one should, rather, have a more positive "faith stance" toward life.

Ponder such nits a bit.

A couple of other unpicked nits are not totally unrelated: what, really, is profanity? What is obscenity?

Get ready, because we're about to get real picky here.

We've a feeling that a lot of folks who get out of joint about words like "gosh" and "golly" don't register a similar moral outrage over such things as this country's bombing of Libya and the killing of innocent children; or our skyrocketing imposition of the death penalty; or the actions of our United States-supported "contras" in

Nicaragua, those counter-revolutionaries whose record of rape, torture, and murder of innocent civilians has been well documented.

There's no doubt about it: words are important, and one should be cautious not to offend with one's speech. But we suggest that as individuals, and as a nation that boasts of being "under God," the greater "taking in vain" of God's name—and the greater profanity and obscenity—is expressed far more tragically in our deeds than in our words.

We'll settle any time for being judged on our words instead of our deeds.

Pick on, nitpickers. The fields are white unto harvest. Just go for the big ones first.

A Tough Problem

We've got a tough problem in this country. How to regain a lost sense of responsibility.

Some will resist the suggestion, contending we never had such a sense in the first place. "No sense of responsibility? So what else is new?" is the response.

But the issue of a damaged, if not lost, sense of individual and corporate responsibility remains. One need only reflect on current instances of dishonesty in government, immorality among religious personalities, and financial highjinks by prominent business executives to know all is not well with our national sense of responsibility.

A frequently heard response in the Iran-contra hearings reflects the problem: "I was just following orders. I work for somebody else."

It's not a new problem, of course. It's as old as the Garden of Eden and as recent as the holocaust, Watergate, Irangate, and Pearlygate.

We may be dreaming, but we seem to recall that once upon a time this country could boast of individuals and groups who cared for the well-being of the whole, whose sense of corporate responsibility both restrained and motivated them. But woe is us; such days seem a distant memory.

Our point herein is simple: the problem of a lost sense of responsibility—especially moral responsibility—is of particular significance to this country's religious community. The problem, though not solely the burden of the church and synagogue, is a special responsibility of those whose daily duty requires them to speak of such things as morality, ethics, and righteousness.

Perhaps that's the problem—that so many Americans, from common folks to top leadership, seem content only to speak about, rather than to embody, principles of morality and ethics.

Today's homily plows no new ground: the world is made better not by hearing sermons, but by seeing them.

Again, there's the squeak—being moral, rather than just using the rhetoric of morality—is no easy task. We could wish it were otherwise, but it's not.

Calls to "return to morality" are not without their dangers. All sorts of legalities and hypocrisies, including bigotry and fascism, lurk close behind such admonitions.

But the need is real and the burden remains. Where are those homes, those parents, those leaders in religion and government who will help this nation regain its damaged sense of moral responsibility?

The fields are white unto harvest. Have the laborers migrated?

The Inferior Ones

Look, we've gotta talk. There's some heavy stuff I need to unload.

But there's a problem. To be honest, well, I'm sort of afraid to reveal this. It's kind of personal and, you might say, I'm timid. No, I'm scared.

I suspect I'm the only person in the whole world ever to feel this way. However, on the outside chance that there just might be a couple of you out there who've this same problem, I'll go ahead and tell all.

Inferiority complex.

There, I've said it. That's my problem. It's this nagging feeling of not being adequate to the occasion, not measuring up to other folks' expectations. It's the feeling of being inferior.

I even had a dream about this. I went to talk to an expert. I sat down, told my depressing story, and this is what the expert said: "John, it's simple. You're inferior."

I want a second opinion, I said.

"Okay," the expert replied, "here it is. John, you're way below average and your mother dresses you funny."

So much for help from experts.

But hang on, fellow inferiorities—if indeed there are any others of you out there. There's help at hand.

This particular bit of help comes in a rather cryptic way. I ran across it in a book by psychiatrist and author Dr. M. Scott Peck. In the prelude of his new book, *The Different Drum*, Dr. Peck recounts an old story, origin unknown.

It seems there was a small group of monks, the remnant of an ancient, once successful monastery that now faced extinction. The old abbot, despondent over the impending demise of his monastery, sought comfort from a respected friend, an aged rabbi.

The rabbi, himself the spiritual leader of a diminishing flock, also was in search of hope for the future.

"What help can you give me?" the abbot asked.

The rabbi thought long and then spoke. The abbot, unsure about the rabbi's strange message, returned to his monks.

"The rabbi said he couldn't help," the abbot reported. "We just wept and read the Torah together. The only thing he did say, just as I was leaving—it was something cryptic—was that the Messiah is one of us. I don't know what he meant."

"I have no advice to give," the old rabbi had said. "The only thing that I can tell you is that the Messiah is one of you."

The monks, who had known each others' faults for years, couldn't imagine any one of their associates being, of all things, the Messiah!

But in time, a strange thing began to happen. The monks gained greater respect for each other and for themselves individually. The idea that one of them could be the Messiah had affected them so profoundly that the whole atmosphere of the once demoralized monastery changed.

New recruits were attracted and soon the monastery flourished, all because of the transformation wrought by the rabbi's gift.

So, my dear little inferior ones, take heart. I have it on good authority: one of you out there is the Messiah.

The Trouble with Sin

We've been sitting here through two cups of hot chocolate trying to figure out something religious to write about. A bunch of topics have come to mind:
- Tithing.
- Women's Missionary Society meetings.
- Choir robes.
- Sunday school picnics.
- Sin.

Not, at the moment, feeling inspired to say anything new or uplifting about the first four of those topics, we have decided to choose No. 5, the all-around American favorite.

So, here we go. Our topic for the day is sin. S-i-n.

But we've got a couple of problems. First, what's new or uplifting that can be said about sin? Frankly, we don't know. But, as we frequently are reminded, ignorance of a subject never stopped us from writing about it.

There's another problem. The trouble with sin these days is that most folks have the wrong idea about what it is.

Mention the word sin and most folks immediately start thinking X-rated thoughts—stuff about sex and things like that.

Some aspects of sex can, doubtless, qualify for the sin category. But real sin—good old Bible sin—has to do with a lot more than what are called "matters of the flesh."

Honest-to-goodness sin, really first-class sin, most often comes disguised, dressed in sheep's clothing.

For example, authentic sin, rather then having to do with sex and stuff, is more likely to reveal itself in such things as our attitudes towards others, in actions designed to put our own welfare above our neighbor's.

Modern sin has to do with individuals and governments that lie, with officials who say one thing and mean another, with big nations that inflict their own will on small nations. Grown-up sin has to do with principalities and powers in high places that inflict injustices on the poor.

Contemporary sin has to do with social structures and governmental policies that keep the powerless in their place, that sustain unjust systems.

Up-to-date sin has to do with the desecration of God's good earth and air and seas. Modern sin has to do with profit motives that run roughshod over the common good.

Big-boy sin has to do with the religious groups that preach a prosperity gospel while millions go without.

Genuine sin has to do with preachers who proclaim a self-centered salvation and practice wheel-and-deal economics to fill their offering plates.

Sin in this modern day has to do with our refusal to know our enemies, with selfishness that keeps our fists clenched tight on our many possessions while masses perish for want of a morsel.

It would be nice if sin weren't so annoying, so intrusive.

But that's the way it is with sin.

Have a nice day.

A Pretty Good Deal

The other week when the whole sky seemed to be falling—world economies in shambles, increasing conflict in the Persian Gulf, the Cardinals' loss of the World Series—a pleasant distraction arrived at our desk.

We were given an offer we're finding hard to refuse:

"$100 worth of beauty care for only one cent!"

At first we didn't know whether to take offense at the inference—who says we need beauty care?—or to rejoice that we had been favored with such a bonanza. We opted for the latter.

It sounds like a pretty good deal. Any time you can beautify the world around you for only a penny, go for it.

The topic is a religious one, of course. Beauty is very much one of God's favorite subjects. God likes beauty. Beauty was God's idea in the first place. God created beauty.

It's interesting, though. God's idea of beauty is probably a whole lot different from what obsesses contemporary society. We moderns tend to think of beauty as having to do with exterior things—with "prettiness" or handsomeness.

Mind you, we're not against prettiness. We've seen what the world calls ugly and we've seen pretty and we like pretty better.

But here's the point: some of the most beautiful people we've known would never qualify for anybody's "pretty" contest.

Pretty is skin deep. Beauty is quite another thing.

Beauty has to do with a bunch of things that have nothing in common with handsome or pretty. Beauty has to do with such things as authenticity, openness, empathy, acceptance, kindness, forgiveness, tolerance, compassion, and gentleness and, at the same time, firmness.

Beauty has to do with truth, justice, equality, conviction, integrity, honor.

Beauty has to do with love.

The idea intrigues: "$100 worth of beauty care for only one cent!"

Herewith our own idea of a hundred bucks (or more) worth of beauty care for our much abused world (and it won't cost you a bundle):

■ More awareness of each others' needs—more of us

willing to listen, to help, to give, to suffer with one another.

■More tender, loving care for the environment—that we nurture our forests rather than clear-cutting them or using them for military maneuvers; that we clean up our streams, rivers, and lakes; that we purify our air by putting an end to the causes of acid rain and other man-made pollutants.

■Greater harmony among nations—that we celebrate, rather than fear, our differences; that we live and let live; that we seek the common good rather then selfish interest.

There you have it—our one-cent special for the day. It's guaranteed to bring a lot of beauty to this haggard planet.

(You don't even have to send us the penny. Your credit is good.)

By Golly, I'm Tired

Oh, by golly, I'm tired. I'm bone tired.

I'm tired of pushin' this boulder up this hill every week.

I'm tired of strugglin' for social justice.

I'm tired of fightin' the good fight for peace.

I'm tired of beatin' the drum for lost causes like civil rights and capital punishment and clean water and pure air and purer foreign policy.

To heck with all this save-the-world stuff. I'm tired.

And to heck with poor people. To heck with the world's dirty, starving people. They don't smell good. I'd a whole lot rather spend my time with nice, clean people, people who belong to the same social class as I do. Preferably college-educated white people who go to the same church I do, belong to the same political party I do, enjoy the same kind of movies I do. People who are always polite.

Let somebody else save the world. I'm tired. I'm bailing out. I quit. Just leave me alone.

Aha. Now that I'm free from all those burdens, I think I'll take me an extended vacation, do all those things I've always wanted to do.

First off, I'll sail to the South Seas, spend a few months on a deserted island.

Ah, that's nice.

Next, I'll go to Disneyland. Always wanted to do that. Maybe spend a month—maybe even a couple of months—ridin' all those rides I've heard about. And I'll probably go out to eat every night, at some expensive place, and take in a show afterwards. What the heck.

Then I think I'll buy me a couple of those fast sports cars, maybe a boat or two and a home in the mountains or on the beach. And I'll probably goof around a lot, go to bed when I feel like it and sleep late every morning.

Ah, the life . . .

Okay—let's quit this stuff and talk straight for a couple of sentences.

Sure, you're tired. Sure, you're sick to death of all the world's problems. Sure, you can't right all the world's wrongs.

But there are a couple of things you can do. You can hang in there and do your bit. You can—to use a phrase I'm really tired of—keep on keepin' on. And if you're as tired as you say you are, you can rest a bit—and then get the lead out and get on with it.

Maybe if enough of us tired folks hang on, we can get the job done. Or some of it, anyway.

Okay?

Always a Band

Well, it happened again. I let a con man get away with my heart. I couldn't help it.

It was the same fellow who's done it before—Professor Harold Hill, that delightfully slick traveling salesman in Meredith Wilson's *The Music Man* who conspires to sell a bunch of nonexistent band instruments to the gullible citizens of River City, Iowa.

Professor Hill, you remember, volunteers to save the town's young people from the evils of the pool hall by promising to organize a band. He convinces the youngsters they can learn to play real music by using "the think system."

(I've always sort of believed that myself.)

Having last week had the delight of seeing the durable musical once again at Murry's Dinner Playhouse, I've had my batteries recharged.

For me, the most delightful aspect of the story is that the con man gets conned by his own game. Professor Hill, who knows there never was a band, hears music in his heart and soul he can neither deny or resist.

The zinger for me is when Professor Hill, his scam revealed, is confronted by one of the youngsters who had placed such great faith in this bogus bandmaster.

"There never was a band, was there?" sobs the broken-hearted youngster.

A now-sincere Harold Hill, grasping the lad by the shoulders and looking straight in his eyes, says with great conviction:

"I always think there's a band, kid!"

Precisely!

Once you've heard the music, you know there has to be a band!

"Preach faith till you have faith" was the counsel given a then-languished John Wesley who, feeling bereft of faith himself, told a wise confidant he was not fit to preach to others.

"I always think there's a band, kid!"

"Preach faith till you have faith!"

I suspect that most of us, if we would be still enough to listen to the music within us, could know there's always a band—no matter how much disappointment we may have experienced or how many challenges life may have hurled at us.

It is, of course, a fact: there is always a band.

Even when life's music is drowned out by the world, somewhere beyond the horizon a band plays.

When pain, sorrow, despair, or grief lays its heavy burden on us, one may hear, if one listens, the marvelous music of life.

There's always a band!

Thank God for the world's music-makers. They are a heavenly band, indeed.

Explorations

Sometimes Mountains

Sometimes when driving the plains—
those long, rolling, interminable spaces—
I think for a fleeting moment
that far off on the dim, distant horizon,
shimmering through heat waves,
I can see mountains.

Mountains!

Abrupt, rugged peaks
rising to where the air is thin
and the tree line is far below
and the snow lies
in undisturbed serenity.

A rushing in my soul.

Sometimes when sleep comes late at night
and through my open window
the breeze hums her lovely melody
I think for a passing moment
that I can hear the wind
racing over some high mountain pass.

I hear it changing key from spruce to aspen
and rushing on
to ruffle hues on mountain meadows
and dapple the face of solitary snow-water lakes.

A quickening in my chest.

Sometimes when the meetings are long
and the speakers drone on and on
I close my mind and open my heart and think

that I can feel the trail under my boots
and my pack deliciously heavy against my back
and my legs straining on the zig-zag climb.

And I look up and know
that the summit is over the ridge above.

A smile on my face and in my heart.

Strange it is with mountains.
They are so very much more than they are.

Compromise
Thoughts during Apollo 8 Week, 1968

The moon was out, too, that night
   when our wise men first chose that famous Star.

In fact, the moon had been out every night
   before that time
     and every night since that time,
      though we hadn't always been able to see it
               from   where   we
               stood.

But now, come next Sunday if all goes well,
   wise men will not only watch for the Star
     this Christmas Eve, but
         will circle the moon
         will circle the moon
         will circle the moon!

How unbelievably, gloriously
   wonderful!

How it should move us beyond awe
and even to reverence
and cause us to be still.
            And to think.
            And to pray.
                    (The moon, indeed,
                    looks bigger
                    than a star.
                    By far.
                    But so does might
                    than right.
                    And so does fear
                    than faith.)

But let it not be said,
    someday in the long
                long
                far away,
        that wise men in our time
            settled for the moon
        when all the while the Star
                    still shone
                    still beckoned
                    still sent its call
                        to wise men
                            to come on up higher.

Lightning from My Cloud
After Watching a Summer Storm at Night

If someday I live on a cloud,
I want to sit up late on summer nights
and watch the lightning dance around the sky.

(I always wanted to do that
when I lived on earth,
but my porch was no cloud
and I could see just enough
to make my soul thirsty
and my heart hungry.

And reluctantly, I would return indoors,
yearning for more of that mysterious,
ever-changing, always teasing lightshow.)

It's not that I want to understand
the lightning's secrets.
I really don't care so much
about its hows and whats.
It is enough that I may ponder its whys

I just want to watch
and marvel
and enjoy.

And, as I take in the show
with all my loved ones around,
I'd like to have some friends over from their cloud.
Together we could share our *ooh*'s and *ah*'s
as we watch the moving mountains
boil and bubble and rumble
and flash in silver and purple
and gray and pink
and black and white
and finally grow quiet
and pass on somewhere
(I do wonder where),
leaving a vast stillness and peace
across the eternal sky.

Afterwards we could fall asleep
and dream of what we have enjoyed together
and wake in time for the next offering.

You're Excused, Marianne

To Marianne, Bafut Midwifery Clinic
Bamenda, Cameroon, West Africa; October 1, 1977

"Seven children died in this ward
weekend-before-last."

. . .

I watched her young Swiss face as she said it.

You do not say, just with your voice, "Seven children
died
in this ward weekend-before-last."

You say it through too-early lines in your face.
You say it with moistened eyes that mirror
an anguish
a pathos
which words in bright sunlight could never, ever,
express.
You say it with your heart and with your soul—
both of which have known too much of what it means
to see
and hear
and feel
little children die.

. . .

"Seven children died in this ward
weekend-before-last."

. . .

"You'll excuse me, please? I must return to my duties."

117

Africa Is a Child

Thoughts at Bafut Midwifery Clinic
Bamenda, Cameroon, West Africa

Africa is a child nestled in her mother's arms.
   Sometimes she laughs
     Sometimes she cries.

   Africa is a mother
     whose eager face is filled with hope.

. . .

Africa is a child cradled on his mother's lap.
   Sometimes he sleeps
     Sometimes he wakes.

   Africa is a mother
     whose whole being says
     "I am afraid of tomorrow."

. . .

Africa is a young man racing up a mountain.
Africa is an old woman hiding in the bush.

. . .

   Africa is a father whose past
     is an ever-beating drum.

   Africa is a mother whose present
     is an anguished cry of despair
       and a poignant shout of hope.

Africa is a child whose future
is a bold
unrelenting
not-to-be-denied
rising sun.

Distant Trumpets

If you listen carefully you can hear
the sound of distant trumpets.

And the feathery, implacable thunder
of angels' wings, hovering in mighty host
beyond the far horizon, may be distinguished
by the sensitive ear.

The sound of valley being exalted
and mountain made low
begins its vibrations upon the heart.

The whole creation awaits with eager longing
the revealing of the Son of God!

The season is at hand to mark the fullness of time.
It is time to prepare for His coming.

It is Advent!

It has always seemed strange to the world that amidst
all of its sound and fury and in the confusion of its loud
roar, these prior sounds should prevail. But prevail
they do.

And they come as eternal hope.

They declare that goodwill and peace will triumph.
They foretell that spear and sword will give way to
plowshare and pruning hook and that the sobbings of
war will be overcome by the shoutings of peace.

So we begin now our journey to Bethlehem. And
how dear is the goal of our venture! No word short of
"Salvation!" has been able to express what persons
have found beneath the hovering wings and before the
sounding trumpets.

And how welcome these sounds are!
"Like cold water to a thirsty
soul
is good news from a far country."

Beyond Good Friday

*Death, be not proud, though some
have called thee mighty and dreadful,
for thou are not so. . . .
Death, thou shalt die.*
—*John Donne (1573-1631)*

Dead, they said.
On a cross.
From nails. And a spear in his side
and thorns in his head. And people.

Dead.

But dead is something that happens to things. Not to
persons. Not to ideals and dreams and vision and
truth and love.
And certainly not to him.

So they may tell me that He is dead but I will
not believe them. Not just because I do not want
to believe them and not because I came in on the
story later than they did and have seen the whole
thing from the other side of the tomb.

But I will not believe them
because dead men do not still live
and because dead men do not still dream
and cry and laugh and run and touch
and suffer and dance and listen
and hunger and give and love.

And all these things
he did just this morning.

. . .

So when they come with their tale that
he is dead and show me the empty cross
and the sealed tomb and the torn veil
and say to me that it is all over
I will not believe them.

I will ask only that they wait two days
and then run and run and run and shout whatever
message they then may possess.

Return to a Birthing Place

So far gone
   in some distant past,
     light-years away,
   that it may be
     only dimly recalled.

. . .

Washington Elementary School.
Early Fall heavy in the air.
   Feet crowded, uncomfortable
    in shoes infrequently worn
    since last the bell rang in Spring.

An open window.
   Trees red and yellow
     and
    A bird flying free
    Calls to me
    To come and see . . .

But the teacher says
   "Today, we read from Kipling."

. . .

And other windows open—
   and even the birds and trees
   gather close to listen.
    And they travel with me
     on journeys lands away.

. . .

And in a voice no one hears,
   The doctor says,
    "It's a boy."

Stolen Joy
On Watching at the Airport

I saw you all,
   waiting at the airport,
   watching each face come 'round the corner.

I knew
   almost as soon as you,
   when your soldier husband, daddy, and son
   came next in sight!

How you flew into each other's arms!

And—as I stole your joy for my own—
   I watched him close his eyes
   as he held each of you so very close,
   quiet for a moment
    as if to savor a long-nourished dream.

   How tender your greeting.
    How moving to watch your faces.
     How beautiful your tears.
    How delightful your laughter.

(I wondered if you could see my eyes, brim full,
   or could hear my heart
    or feel what I felt in my throat.)

. . .

I wish those who despair of love
could go to the airport
and sit a spell.

Full Circle
Why Grown Men Must Play

At times I think I must have been right
    when I was a child
to believe that I could do grown-up things
    better than grown-ups could.

And now that I am an adult
    I mourn my lost childhood wisdom
        and certainty
        and confidence.

            Where did they go?
            Why do I not now have that assurance
                that children own?

But one thing I do know for certain
    now that I am grown:
        I can do children's things now
            much better than they can!

        And that is good.

        And that, somehow, better equips me
        for the adult things I know I must be about.

Among Other Things

Among other things, God sends rainy days
    to water the garden of our soul,
to nourish the frail, gentle plots
    where the heart-food grows.

God gives the long, slow rains
    to strengthen our poet,
        our philosopher
who cannot live by fair weather alone.

God delivers the thunder to shake up
    our barrel of thoughts—
        to bring to the top what we have let
            work to the bottom,
        to mulch the rich and sweet and pungent
            with the ordinary,
                enriching the whole.

God's lightning reveals truths so radical
    we can stand only the momentary,
        fleeting glimpse.

And God's son comes as benediction.
And as prelude.
        Warming us.
            Toasting us.
                Growing us.
    Among other things.

And Then There Was Mars

A summer collage on Joy and Wonder and Rebirth and Hope

They've written poems about thunder
    and about clouds
        and about summer evenings
    and sunrises
    and about children's laughter
        and a son's tears
        and a father's crying
    and about a mother's strength.

And songs have been sung about love
        and about life
    and about dying and being born
    and about losing and winning
        and suffering and joy
    and good and evil
        and about everything
        and about nothing.

They've painted pictures of kittens
    and courthouses
    and tall ships at sea
    and wild horses
        and angry mobs
    and starving children
    and the rich and the poor
and the passionate and the uncaring.

And they've made stories about hot days
        and cool nights
    and about the wind
        and the pine trees
    and about the eagle and the moon
        and the stars.

And now about Mars.

I thought they had told and sung and painted
and written of everything that stirs and moves
and thrills and hurts
    and joys me so.

        And now there is Mars.
So again I may make my music
    and do my poems
        and tell my tales
    and paint my pictures.

And I know that I must sail the seas
    and walk the mountains
        and do my own dance upon summer clouds
    and lift every stone upon my hill.

        And I will sit in my treehouse
        and watch the turkey buzzards soar.

        And I'll look off towards Mars,
            and smile.

Found Is the Hunter

I searched for those things
that make me "me,"
I looked to the earth
and the sky and the sea.

I ventured on journeys,
lost in my dreams,

to places not traveled
though clearly seen.

I walked through the snows
of deep December,
I fished in a Book
and tried to remember.

I relived a morning
early in Spring,
I followed a bird
high on the wing.

I felt the West wind
full in the sail,
pursuing a vision
of the Holy Grail.

I climbed in a tree,
the family kind,
and pondered the mystery
of the Mind divine.

I studied people
and rummaged through thoughts,
I considered the "dos"
and weighed the "oughts."

I repented of things
that were left undone,
of battles lost
and victories won.

And I lived in love
where I made my home,
but remained content
that my search go on.

At the last I'll know,
when I inherit my ground,
that while I was searching
I was being found.

Something with My Heart

I was always going to make something with my hands,
 something for a special occasion,
 and give it to those I love the best.
Something small, not especially useful.
Something with more soul in it than sense.

But time has a way of running.
And we have a way of putting time aside,
 thinking that it, too, will wait.

But if too late with work of hand,
 not—I should hope—too late
with work of heart, and of soul.

For sometimes the finer work is to fashion
a gift with the heart and deliver it upon
 the simple, written word.

And so, dear friend of mine,
 here is my gift of heart.

This is for you.

Peregrinations

Two Things I Always Wanted

You should come over to my house one of these evenings and see my fireplace. It's a whole lot like other fireplaces, I suppose, but it's mine. And it's something I always wanted.

And if you don't care about seeing my fireplace, you can come over and see my new personal computer. It's probably like most other personal computers you've seen, but it's mine. And it's something I've wanted for about the past dozen or more years.

And if you don't care about seeing my computer, then you can just come on over and we'll drink hot chocolate or coffee or tea or whatever else you may want that's legal and moral. And we can eat cookies or fudge with pecans from our five pecan trees in them.

Now is that an offer you can't refuse or what?

But since you might not be able to come over anytime soon, let me tell you, right here and now, some more about my fireplace and computer.

It's not as if I've never had a fireplace. I have. But the only other fireplace I've ever had in my entire life is in our family cabin at Mount Magazine, about 90 miles from here. And since we only get there during the summer months, mostly, we really don't get to use it much.

Not so, however, with our fireplace here at home. We use this one about every time the temperature drops below 65 degrees—even if we have to turn on the air conditioner to generate the temperature (not really).

You can count on it: from the first cool day in fall (maybe even in late summer) until the warmest day in spring, the fireplace at our house will be in use. A thing that lets you burn wood inside your house is a joy forever.

Tell me something that's more fun than poking a fire

and I'll tell you something you probably shouldn't be doin'.

There's magic about a fireplace. Most common men, and all common women, become philosophers while sitting before a wood fire at night.

Ordinary church members become top-flight theologians, on a par with those graduates of seminaries and preacher schools, when oak embers warm the body and hardwood smoke seduces the soul.

Show me the person who sits by a fireplace on long winter nights and I'll show you a wise person indeed.

God probably got most of God's really good ideas while sitting before a wood fire at night.

Now about that personal computer of mine (the farthest thing from a wood-burning fireplace that I can imagine)—that's something else I can get excited about.

I don't know a whole lot about this machine, but I do know that it's easier to write on one of these things. As one who once was convinced that nothing could ever be written on an electric typewriter (as compared with the old manual kind), I've had to eat my words about these newfangled apparatuses.

They do, in fact, save a lot of time. The hard work of writing is still here—all the rewriting that has to be done and all that. But the word processor makes it so much easier to correct mistakes, move paragraphs and sentences around, and do all kinds of work that take so long when using a typewriter.

So consider me sold—both on a wood-burning fireplace and a word-processing computer.

The only problem with my two favorite material possessions (my ten-speed bicycle ranks high on such a list) is that they're not in the same room together. My little study (actually a walk-in clothes closet) is too small for my fireplace, and our den, where the fireplace is, is much too public a place for the solitary business that goes on in front of a computer screen.

No moral or religious lessons here—just a bunch of talk. But maybe if you had promised not to read this chapter, the bookstore would have given you a discount.

Sorry—too late now.

"You Writin' Fool"

Here I sit in my study at home, in front of my computer, hooked up to my chemotherapy bottle, into the third day of a four-day chemo treatment and writin' like a fool.

"Workman," I say to myself (I talk to myself a lot during these monthly sessions), "you're a writin' fool!"

"I know," I reply to myself. "I can't help it. But God knows I'm sorry." (That's a line I picked up from Tommy Smothers.)

"Oh, well," I answer, "you Workmans always were sort of funny, if you know what I mean."

The word *fool* is, of course, a rather harsh one. I once read somewhere that newspaper columnists should never use the word *fool* when referring to someone else. The implication was that it was okay for columnists to use the word about themselves.

But whatever, a man's gotta do what a man's gotta do and what I gotta do is write. Or try to—whether like a fool or any other way.

Did you ever stop to think about how many things there are to write about?

I tried to count them once—things there are to write about—but when I got up to 76, I quit. It seemed the end was nowhere in sight so I went back to sleep.

Which, too, is something one could write about—sleep, that is.

That is, one could write about sleep if one couldn't

135

sleep—which is doubtless the better by far of the two activities.

Speaking of writing, there's something I can't figure out just now—whether it's this chemotherapy that's nauseating me, or what I'm writing.

I think I know which it is.

Oh, well, what the hey, as they say.

Why do they always say that? Someone once wrote me a letter at the *Arkansas Gazette* objecting to my use, in a column, of the words "heck" and "gosh," I think it was. The person said that those words were euphemisms for swear words that I, as a paragon of religious virtue, shouldn't be using.

I didn't know about those words. I bet the same thing is true with "hey," as I used it. I sure hope not.

Anyway—back to writing—if any of you authors out there have writer's block, let me suggest that you try my chemo formula. It'll do either of two things for your brain: lock it up and shut it down, or shake it around and turn it loose. There are a bunch of other things it'll do for you, none of which I could recommend to anyone looking for a happy time.

Now, lest you think that these chemicals have turned me completely goofy and that I shouldn't be allowed within twenty feet of a word processor while under the influence, know that during this same four-day treatment, I have composed a couple of newspaper columns, done some carpentry work, polished up a couple of chapters for this book, and generally bothered those around me till they, too, are full ready for this session to be over.

So there.

"Workman," I said to myself, "you're a crazy writin' fool if I ever saw one."

"You'll get no argument from me on that," I replied.

Things Never Done

I surely must be the only human in downtown Little Rock (though there could be three or four others) who didn't see, or even hear, the arrival or the departure last week of the Concorde, that supersonic airplane that seems to be the symbol of all that our modern civilizations should ever aspire to become.

This depressing experience—not seeing the Concorde—came to mind the other day as I read about our governor's having bought several new suits—one reported to have cost upwards of $900— and Tammy Faye Bakker crying in public that she and Jim had only $37,000 to their name (plus a million-dollar parsonage.)

Lo, how the righteous suffer.

The whole depressing business triggered my recall systems, bringing up all those many things I had never, ever possessed or done in my entire life. The list seemed endless.

I have never owned a convertible automobile.

I have never seen *Gone With the Wind.*

I have never climbed to the top of the Empire State Building.

I have never had dinner at the bishop's house (though I once had coffee and doughnuts there).

I have never paid more than $139.98, I think it was, for a suit of clothes—and even when I paid that outrageous price I felt guilty and have never repeated the offense. (My friends tell me they've noticed.)

I have never had fine grape juice on the veranda with any member of Arkansas's famous Good Suit Club.

Although I have had at least three dandy bicycles in my time, I have never paid more than $27 for any of them. Again, my friends have frequently voiced notice of this.

And I have never been a guest on *The 700 Club*, although I have had several invitations to speak in church and once addressed a garden club. Oh, yes—I once gave the invocation at the Carroll County Rodeo.

The list of all the other things I've never, ever done or possessed could fill this newspaper.

But there are, of course, a bunch of neat things I have done.

When our children were young, I got to take them with me when we drove through the automatic car wash machine (it only cost a quarter then). On one such occasion with our youngest, then about four years old, and my only passenger exclaimed, "Oh boy, Daddy, that was fun! Maybe next time we could bring the whole family!" We did.

Also, I have had the joy of lying on my back in a meadow on Mount Magazine, watching buzzards make lazy circles in the sky. No charge.

And once, when attending an out-of-town meeting, I actually got a glimpse of then-Vice President Gerald Ford.

There are other exciting things I've done, but you're probably so worked up about the above you're not up to hearing about them just now. They'll keep.

So, settle down and get on with that ordinary life you're living.

But get ready—you never know when something really exciting, really wonderful, might happen to you.

It could be today.

A Cowboy's Lament

It's confession time in the old corral, pardners. You'll need to get ready for this.

Even my closest loved ones will have to prepare for what I'm about to unload. Here goes:

What I always really wanted to be was a cowboy.

Yep, that's right. I wanted to be a cowboy.

I always wanted to be a real, live, bronco-bustin', calf-ropin', trail-ridin', straw-chewin', Saturday-night-lovin' cowboy.

(Don't pay any attention to the picture in the above left corner—that's not really me. Think John Wayne. Imagine Randolph Scott.)

I always wanted to sip my coffee from a tin cup, sleep under the stars, and listen to the dogies lowin' as the cobwebs filled my head.

I always wanted to rise at the first hint of dawn, rustle up some grub, hit leather before sunup. I always wanted to burn daylight.

I always wanted to ride the range till I lost my senses, till I was so saddle-sore I could hardly move. I always wanted to hunker down by the campfire at night, eat some beans and beef, strum my guitar, play my old harmonica, spit when I wanted to, and maybe even sing a ballad or two.

And aw, shucks, I might as well tell it: I always wanted to carry a six-gun—not to shoot people, of course, but to protect women and children from wild varmints and bad hombres. I was going to be a gentle, strong, tall-in-the-saddle cowboy, the kind whose presence would command respect. Jimmy Stewart, Henry Fonda, and even Clint Eastwood would have wanted to be just like me.

If you're thinking all this stuff is just a bunch of fantasy, you need to be informed of an actual fact: I can, in truth, list "working cowboy" as among my several previous employments, however brief and unremunerative the experience may have been.

The place was Texas (naturally), where I also was posing as a graduate student. I can attest under oath that I actually was employed as "a real cowboy" for most of three whole days and got paid five dollars, I think it was, for "workin' a roundup," as we veteran cowhands used to call it.

Facts: I actually rode the range on a cattle drive. I actually headed 'em up and moved 'em out. I actually ate from an old chuck wagon. I actually slept out under the stars. I actually got saddle-sore.

It didn't take me long to discover I was too much man for their little chicken-feed outfit. I moved on.

So, my surprised friend, know that you're not talkin' to any citified greenhorn here. I've done my time poundin' leather. That's the solitude of wide open spaces you see in these eyes, stranger. Step aside.

Okay, never mind that most real cowboys would have given their last grubstake to be relieved of the misery of their daily lives. Never mind that real cowboyin' was a devilishly hard, bone-jarring, hot, cold, boring, lonely, thankless, God-forsaken existence.

Never mind about all that. We're talking life here, and in life it's the dream that counts. In life it's the romance that matters. In life it's the vision—so much more than the reality—that finally makes the difference.

So come on, all you cowboys and cowgirls, let's hit the trail. There are women and children out there who need rescuin'. There are causes that need some friends. There are strays that need roundin' up, dogies that need tendin' to.

Get your gear together, amigos. It's leather-hittin' time.

As a Sailor

If you liked me as a cowboy, you'll love me as a sailor. (Oh, no, Mabel, it's that silly stuff again. What's happened to this man? Do you suppose he's on something? And anyway, what's all this got to do with anything—and especially with religion? Isn't this book supposed to be about religion?)

Mr. Chairman (we're still in our Iran-contra hearings mode here), we'd like to answer each of those questions. First, no, we're not "on" something. Second, yes, something's happened to us—we've been hit with a bad attack of "the recollections." Only those who've had such onsets will understand. For those who haven't, no amount of explaining will suffice.

And third, what all this has to do with religion is only everything. Be patient.

Now let's get on with it.

It's true, mates. Even before I rode the range as a professional cowhand, I bounded on the bounding main as a sailor—no less than a fully employed, if scantily paid, Able-bodied Seaman. (When I left sailorin' to take up cowboyin' you might say I traded the bounding main for the bounding mane.)

So add one more entry to our growing list of previous employments: "Sailor—Able-bodied Seaman."

Some actual facts: I actually went down to the sea in ships (never mind that it happened to be in Illinois, on Lake Michigan, and that most of the vessels were of the 18- to 26-foot variety.)

I actually knew that left was port and right was starboard. I actually hoisted the mains'l. I actually shouted, "Helm's a-lee!" I actually hiked out to windw'rd and caught spray in the face so cold it made your teeth taste like iron.

I actually waited-out being becalmed. I actually went

almost sunblind staring at glassy seas while our little boat sat dead in the water for what seemed like months.

I actually rode out a bunch of nor'easters. I actually bailed for dear life. I actually was exhilarated as our little craft rode the breakers into harbor, planing on the crest of a breaking wave till the mains'l backed and we risked a jibe.

Another actual fact: I was, for about 22 hours as I recall, a member of the United States Merchant Marine. When my Draft Board got news that I joined the Merchant Marine (after failing the vision test to get into the Navy), the whole United States Army became so enraged at losing me that they cancelled my MM enlistment and honored me with an immediate draft into Uncle Sam's army. I accepted their invitation and served with distinction—yet another story for some rainy evening.

So, mates, know that what you see in this countenance is the tranquility of far horizons, the peace of lazy lagoons in the sunset. Know that this bronzed body, its rippling muscles hardened by fighting many a gale, harbors a heart as peaceful as seagulls in flight.

(Now here comes the religious part. Get ready.)

Life's a voyage. Life's a journey across uncharted depths. Our ship is small and the sea is large. We need a compass. We need a North Star, a Southern Cross.

(Is this religious enough for you? There's more.)

How, O God of all travelers, are humble sailor lads and lassies to find their way to that safe Port beyond the horizon?

What's this? You say that finding the answer to that question is part of the gift of the voyage?

Then let's be at it, mates! All hands on deck. There's a fresh wind quarterin' and our seaworthy little craft has a bone in her teeth.

Sail on!

As A Soldier

Since none of my children or grandchildren ever asked me the question, "What did you do in the war, Daddy (or Grandpaw)?" I'm going to pretend you did.

Thanks for asking. I've been waiting—for about 43 years, in fact.

What I did in the war (the Big WWII, we vets call it) is not for timid ears to hear. What I did in the war is not for the fainthearted to dwell upon. Buckle your seatbelts.

What I Did in the War, by Sgt. John S. Workman, ASN 46040310.

Well, let's see.

Do you mean after I guarded the German troops, at Fort Sheridan, Illinois, on the night of the very first day I was inducted into the service? Those troops were fresh from combat in the deserts of North Africa and were as tough a bunch as you'd ever want to see. The Army people put a uniform on me, stuck a rifle (loaded, I supposed) in my hand, and told me the security of the whole United States of America was on my shoulders for the next eight hours.

I must have done things right because the next morning we Americans were still in control.

That's the first thing I did in the war.

Actually, that was about the third thing I did in the war.

The first thing I did in the war was to get a haircut—or rather be given a haircut. It was one of those real haircuts, the kind I had to wait about another fifteen years to grow into naturally.

The second thing I did in the war was to take off all my clothes, put on an ice-cold raincoat, stand in line outdoors in the freezing rain for about an hour, and wait for the joy of being given a physical exam and about 80 shots.

General Sherman told the truth about war.

Or do you mean by your question "What did you do in the war, John?" what I *really* did in the war?

Well, one of the really real things I did in the war was on the island of Iwo Jima, some months after the infamous battle on Mount Suribatchi. It was there that I almost became one of the very last casualties of WW II.

It happened this way.

Our plane, en route to Okinawa, landed at Iwo Jima for an overnight stay. We were told to remain near our quarters because there were still hostile Japanese soldiers hiding in caves throughout the island.

No problem. I had already decided, after hearing their little talk, to stay near, very near—in fact as near as you could possibly get—to my quarters. I had decided to stay so near to the safety of my quarters that they would have to pry me loose to get me even to answer chow call.

Only in order to get to the quarters I was to share with a half-dozen other GIs, we had to walk through a dark and scary bit of jungle. I was last in line, having volunteered to guard our dangerous rear flank.

About halfway to our Quonset hut, along that dark, scary trail, a form suddenly lurched out of the jungle, jumped squarely on my shoulders, and grabbed me around the neck!

"This is it, John!" I thought, as my heart pounded. The picture flashing in my mind: "Right now there's a Western Union boy preparing to get on his bicycle to pedal to your parents' door, John. Sad. Sad, indeed. He was such a fine young man. Such promise."

What I thought was a crazed enemy soldier turned out to be some GI's pet monkey, trained, I suspected, to scare greenhorns like me.

Believe me, it worked. I think it took about three weeks for my heartbeat to get back to normal.

But back to your question about what I did in the war. Do you mean what I really-and-truly did in the war?

Oh, that.

That, as a matter of fact, was so unbelievable that I must refrain from telling you. I'll give you this hint: there were only eight of us in the whole Pacific Theater trained to do what we did. We did it in a secret, remote spot along the border between North and South Korea, and members of our group would rotate between similar sites in China and an island in the South Pacific. We sent weekly officer-couriers to Washington with the results of our work, and we had the Number One Priority, as a unit, to "get the heck out of South Korea" in the event that the North Koreans made a move in our direction.

So, you can imagine that what I really did in the war is worth hearing about. But I've already over-stayed my welcome in this chapter, so you'll just have to wait until the next book.

Sorry. But believe me, it'll be worth the waiting.

Dark, Stormy Night

If you think it takes a long time to spend the night at your house, you ought to try sleeping in the Gazette Building.

I did that the other snowbound evening—tried to sleep at the *Gazette*. And, as a matter of fact, it worked. I actually got some sleep. Not much, but some.

My little adventure was precipitated, of course, by The Great Blizzard of '88—of which you have, by now, already heard enough.

But you need to know about my adventures, if for no other reason than to give me the satisfaction of sharing my suffering.

Living at Conway, 33 miles from home to office, I long ago devised Snow Plan No. 1—what to do in the event of The Big Storm.

Tuesday evening came and it seemed that, after putting up with a whole bunch of sissy winters, my long wished-for great storm was actually in the making. Time to initiate SP No. 1. Hot dog!

I can't remember being so excited since our last family camping trip to Colorado.

As I assembled my gear—almost all of my camping, bicycling, and trail hiking stuff with the exception of my tent, Coleman stove, and survival saw—my packs made the High Mountain Rangers look like novices. I was ready.

I was so ready, in fact, that I had trouble sleeping Tuesday night—and I hadn't even left the comforts of home. Early Wednesday morning, as I prepared to brave the elements, my wife noted my excitement and told me that if the storm didn't materialize and I had to drive home without getting the adventure out of my system, I could set up my campsite in our living room.

That helped.

Once at the Gazette Building, I put my bid in early for the couch in the third-floor office where Arkansas Traveler Charlie Allbright and Our Towner Richard Allin hang out. I frequently had observed that those chaps live rather regally.

(To my disappointment, throughout the day numerous executives around here assured me I didn't have to camp out—that, like the smart people here, I could walk one block to a luxury hotel where, at the Gazette's expense, I could have a real bed, a shower, genuine meals and all that worldly stuff. I told them that would spoil my fun.)

By 9:00 p.m. I was bedded down. I imagined myself camped under the lee of a high, windy ridge, the distant howls of coyotes echoing eerily off the snowy canyon walls. Great!

Somewhere around 2:00 a.m. I awoke. Noting that the bright hallway lights were still on, I wondered if I dared make the 100-foot dash down the hallway to the men's room clad only in my pajamas.

I imagined the conversation of the cleaning crew: "What was that?"

"My, my, I don't know. For a moment it looked like that Reverend Workman, the religion man. But surely not. Anyway, those were pretty pajamas—although that sure was a funny-looking sleeping cap."

By 4:00 a.m. or so, after I had completed my recitation, by memory, of the total content of the first four books of the Old Testament, I was struck by a sudden revelation.

It dawned on me that somewhere in the Bible (I could look it up but I'm too sleepy right now), it is stated that one can't be anywhere that God is not. Or something like that.

If I understand that correctly, it means that God, too, was spending the night in the Gazette Building. This realization did not do a lot for my appreciation of Divine wisdom.

But anyway, it's a nice thought, a handy one for almost any need.

At the moment it appears that I may have a second night of camping to do at the *Gazette*. I think I'm up to it. But if God is as smart as I've always been taught to believe, I may have to spend this one alone.

Opera Phantom

If all goes as planned, by the time you read this my wife and I will be visiting family members in New York and New Jersey.

There's a twofold reason for our trip: to hear our youngest son, a student at The Juilliard School's American Opera Center, sing in an opera; and to visit our

147

oldest son and his wife and their eighteen-month-old daughter, our third grandchild.

Although I'm pretty much burnt out on going to operas, I'll have to admit I'm excited by all this. And, naturally, any parents and grandparents worth their salt would put on their Sunday best, leave home, abandon all responsibilities, and fly away to the big city to take in such activities.

Which is what we have done.

(I can't remember how long it's been since we had a son sing in an opera at New York City. It's been a while.)

Only there's a problem. I've been worrying about what I'll wear to the opera. We don't get too many operas up in Faulkner County, where I live, and I'm having a difficult time recollecting just what everybody wore to the last one we had. Only I can't remember the last one we had.

Our son told us it was "mighty cold" at New York and said we should dress accordingly. But my old topcoat is the coldest garment ever made, and the only really warm coat I have is a hand-me-up from our opera star. It is, without a doubt, the warmest coat I ever lucked in to.

But there's another problem. This really warm coat is shorter than my Sunday suit coat (and my dressy sport coats, too), and when I wear it as a topcoat over my suit it looks a bit nerdy, if you know what I mean.

So I can either go to the opera frozen stiff or I can go looking like a warm nerd from Arkansas—the latter of which choices being what I absolutely intend to do. What's more, I plan to wear my wool stocking hat, the one that covers my ears and my entire head, which is totally bereft of hair. (I can take my coat and hat off about a block before we get to the opera house.)

All of which thoughts inspire some religious reflections.

Most of us worry more about our appearance than we do the state of our souls.

Most of us are more concerned that we might offend the social codes than that we might displease the Almighty.

Most of us are more concerned with form that substance.

Perhaps my going to the opera in my nerdy coat and hat will help correct all this for the entire City of New York and surrounding areas. I just hope they're ready for it.

Oh, well. At least our son won't have any trouble spotting me in the audience. I'll be the one with the stocking hat and the short overcoat and, with luck, my granddaughter on my knee.

And I'll be the one with the brightest, most shining look of pride of any of the millions of people who I know are going to be there to hear our son sing.

Watch out, New York. Here comes the real phantom of the opera.

The Championship Lunch Sack

My wife, Liz, who is always suggesting topics for my weekly newspaper column, says she cannot remember a single time I accepted one of her suggestions. This is for her.

One day recently while preparing my lunch to take to the office, Liz got the paper lunchsack I've been using daily for about the past four months, noticed it needed a change of oil, and commented, "Now here's something you *really* ought to write about—this championship lunchsack."

She just might be right. I may be the owner of the most championship lunchsack in the whole country and I don't even know it. And who knows, I might be

149

the championship lunchsack owner in the whole universe, though surely that would be an honor not so easily attained.

If, indeed, I am the owner of the championship lunchsack, part of the credit must go to Andy's, the fast food establishment that was the original owner of my favorite sack. I got it there with, as I recall, an Andy's-cheese-with-everything-no-fries-and-to-go-please.

That was fully four months ago, perhaps even longer.

Now, every weekday since that time, my faithful Andy's sack has been carrying my lunch. The only addition to its natural beauty is my name boldly inscribed with a Magic Marker, to discourage any would-be lunchnappers who might be tempted.

It figures, I guess. Anybody who would have a desktop that looks like mine does, and whose storeroom looks like mine does, and who collects empty coffee cans and other stuff the way I do surely would use a lunchsack for as long as it could possibly survive.

I suspect you know the type. A lot of you are probably even married to one.

Psychologists and those kinds of experts could probably tell us a lot about people like this, people who use old lunchsacks until they're threadbare, or fiberbare or whatever it is that overused lunchsacks become.

The topic is a natural, of course, for moral-makers, another marginal group in which I also must confess membership.

The using-the-same-ole-lunchsack syndrome has something to do, I suppose, with this throwaway society in which we are all conspirators. We live in the age of planned obsolescence, in which products are designed to break down so we'll have to buy others.

We live in the garbage-can age, when the amount of stuff we throw away daily—food, paper, metal, glass, clothing, cars, and you name it—far surpasses the throwaway habits of any previous society.

Perhaps by using the same lunchsack for a half-year or more, one can register a protest, however mild, to such wasteful ways.

Perhaps the lunchsack preservation phobia also has something to do with the fact that lunchsacks are made out of trees and trees are living things that have to be killed in order for people to read newspapers and books so advertisers can advertise and people like me can have jobs and carry our lunches in sacks that used to be part of a lovely, living, oxygen-producing creation of God.

Progress is probably a good thing, but it so frequently comes at too great a price.

Show me the person who uses a brand-new paper lunchsack every day and I'll show you a person who's wasting our precious forests.

There's another factor relevant to the using-the-same-lunchsack phobia. It has to do with the way one regards oneself.

It feels good to be a conserver. It feels good to know that by placing a brick in the tank of your bathroom commode you are conserving water. It feels good to know that by taking your own shopping bag to the supermarket you are doing a tiny bit to protest the wanton harvest of trees in order to make more paper sacks in order to make more money.

It feels good when, at lunchtime each weekday, you open the office refrigerator and find your old friend, your faithful lunchsack, waiting for you, silently making its statement about the virtues of the frugal and simple life.

So, let no person ever tell you, "It's only an old lunchsack." To the contrary—it's a tree. It's a wilderness striving to survive.

So, we've made it for four months now with our Andy's lunchsack. Let's go for five. And then—who knows?—maybe six. Maybe more.

151

Not Necessarily So

It's not necessarily so.

"If you have your health, you have everything."

There was a time when I believed that. That was when I "had my health." Now that I "don't have my health"—I'm what's commonly thought of as a cancer patient—I'm not so sure about the evaluation.

Some who have their health may, indeed, "have everything."

Others may not. Some who don't have their health may, in fact, feel more blest than the most physically fit among us.

Don't get me wrong. I've been well and I've been sick and I like well a bunch better. For 59 of my 60 years, I enjoyed robust health. I've been a runner and a long-distance cyclist and have lived a vigorous outdoor life.

However, within the last ten months, I've had major surgery and a full course of radiation and currently am at the midpoint of a year-long chemotherapy program that involves four days of treatment each three weeks.

I know—you're tired of reading about this. I am, too, but I need to make a point.

The other evening, I read a book about a fellow who walked across the United States—two times, no less! —to promote the idea that people ought to take care of their bodies. It's a noble cause, a stimulating book, and I found it at the right time.

Since I can't quite sit on my bicycle seat yet, and since I'm not up to running, I've been looking for some kind of physical activity to challenge my body and spirit.

Why not walking?

An excellent idea. The only problem is that while I'm undergoing this chemo, it's about all I can do to walk from my bed to the bathroom. And during the couple of weeks between treatments, an evening stroll of a half-dozen blocks is all I can muster.

But hey, things are getting better.

Before my illness, I had planned to celebrate my 60th birthday with one of my super bicycle tours—a ride completely around the borders of Arkansas. Now another plan is brewing in my mind: why not celebrate my 61st birthday with a several-days-long backpacking expedition at one of my favorite spots on earth, the high Rocky Mountains in Colorado?

Why not!

So, my mind is at work on such a plan. It only awaits the cooperation of the flesh.

Now, the point: the body is a terrible thing to waste. The Creator knows this, which is why, I suspect, we humans are such resilient beings.

So, all you out there who are supposed to have "lost your health," don't you believe it! There are many things you can do, though they may not be great physical feats.

Life is out there, waiting for us. Let's go for it!

Some Good, Some Bad

I'm fixin' to make your day with the kind of Truth in Media you haven't been afflicted with in months, maybe ever.

I'm feeling terrible. Lousy. In fact, I've been feeling so bad I probably shouldn't be allowed within ten feet of one of these machines that jumps your innermost thoughts smack on to the pages of a newspaper.

But I figure there's a whole bunch of you out there who are feeling just as terrible as I do at the moment, perhaps even worse (if that's possible.) So maybe we can feel bad together.

The reason with my current disaffection with the world can be briefly stated: I'm just coming off one of my chemotherapy bouts, which I get to enjoy about every three to four weeks. During this current session, I spent almost all of the four days in bed, trying to keep count of the times (pardon me for this) that I—as we said as children—upchucked. Gratefully, even the Truth in Media code prohibits me from telling you more about that.

I also lost a bit more weight than usual during this bout—ten pounds. Most of that I will put back on before the next session. But it occurred to me that if I didn't regain the weight I lose during these treatments, by the time I was through with all this, in about eight or so more months, I would weigh about seventeen pounds.

Okay, by now you've got the message: I'm feeling tough. Terrible. Lousy. Awful.

What I've just done above is to follow the advice of some good folks who try to help people like me. Social workers say that if you hurt, talk about it, tell it like it is. (That's going to cramp my style—I've always kind of enjoyed telling it a bit worse than it is.)

But hold on, fellow sufferers. That's not all these good people tell us.

They also tell us that after you've griped and got the bad feelings out of your system, it helps to count the good things in your life.

So, now a bit of that.

The good things in my life:

It's been four whole workdays now since somebody parked in my reserved slot.

There is not one single hangnail on any of my ten fingers.

The paint on my house is not peeling.

There's not one television evangelist, so far as I know, who is likely to be in really big trouble within the next couple of weeks.

Enough fun for a while.

There really is a lot of good news around these days. Two bits come to mind, in spite of all the above: life is good, very good; and God hasn't quit the job.

Three Things I Don't Like

Okay, let's get this out of the way right up front.

There are three things I don't like. I don't like to talk about illness. I don't like to read about illness. And most of all, I don't like to write about illness—especially when it's my own.

But that's just what I'm fixin' to do—write about illness. I promise this won't take long, and then both of us, you and I, can get on with this business of living.

By the way, first let me give you, in seven short words, my whole philosophy about being sick: I simply don't have time for it.

There's too much to do to waste time being sick. There are too many things to see, too many places to go, too many times I want to visit with my family, too may chores to tend to, too many bicycle trips to make, too many books to read, too many doo-dads to create, too many mountains to climb, too many sunsets to watch, and too many words to write.

So, illness, get out of my way. I'm hankerin' to get on with life.

Okay—now about illness.

The obvious: illness does some terrible things to us. It makes us hurt. It frightens us. It brings tears. It takes the control of our lives out of our hands. It tests our faith—and it can, let's admit it, make us angry at God.

Just ask Job.

The week that these words were written marks the thirteenth month since I was diagnosed as having cancer. It marks the first anniversary of my surgery, during which the surgeons removed a basketball-sized (their word) tumor from my pelvic region.

I've had the maximum-allowable (for my case) radiation treatments (30) and have had about eight months of chemotherapy, with about four more of those four-day treatments (one session each three to four weeks) to go. So, if all goes well, the conclusion of that long, seemingly endless series of "four fun-filled days," as I've called them, is in sight. Hallelujah!

Now, some not-so-obvious things about illness.

To have such a bad reputation, illness can, in fact, do some rather good things for us. (That's really tough to admit, but a man's gotta admit what a man's gotta admit.)

First off, illness can, if we will let it, give us a renewed appreciation of life. Illness gets our attention. It sharpens our senses. It puts things in perspective.

There's a strange way in which illness and suffering, after they've had a chance to do their work, can give one a renewed enthusiasm for living.

A needed note here: I would not make light of the battles fought by those who hurt and have no respite from pain and misery. I couldn't have written the above three paragraphs some ten or so months ago when I was hurting, afraid, bereft of faith, and frightened near to the point of despair.

(So, to you fellow sufferers who at this moment are in the throes of pain and despair, know that others understand. Know, too, that others have been there and have had the experience of grace working its miracles.)

For now, let's both of us—you and me—hang on and get on with living. We've no time for illness. We've no time, even, for sleep. Only the dead sleep. There's too much going on out there. Let's not miss it.

And remember—grace can break through at any moment.

Be ready.

A Box for You

At supper the other evening I told my wife and my mother that I was reminded of a prank Hendrix College üpperclassmen used to play on freshmen—and that I had been one of those freshmen.

But hold on a minute. It you're going to appreciate (that may not be the right word) all this, you need to know that I have just completed another four-day chemotherapy treatment, hopefully the last in a year-long monthly series.

The supper I refer to was the first meal I had attempted in three days. I had lost twelve pounds during those three days, thanks (another questionable word) to all the prolonged and violent abdominal activity that goes with chemotherapy.

If you're still with me, I'll continue. This gets worse.

"Just call John McNutt and tell him to go ahead on and bring the box," I muttered between attempts to do what one is supposed to do with an omelette.

"What did you say?" my hard-of-hearing mother, still sweet at 88, asked. The name of John McNutt, our long-deceased Conway funeral director, had caught Mother's attention. Mr. McNutt, a family friend, was your real-life, honest-to-goodness friendly undertaker and solid citizen.

"Just tell John McNutt to go ahead and bring the box," I said again, remembering the Hendrix prank.

That prank, as I now recall some 40 years later, occurred in about my second week in Martin Hall, the Hendrix dorm where a lot of us freshmen were stored. We were put under the protective care of much-trusted upperclassmen, stalwart men all, whose sole interest in life was the welfare of their young charges.

The note appeared on the hall chalkboard: "Work-man: call 222. They have a box for you." Naturally, visions of goodies from home filled my head.

The 222 number was, of course, that of McNutt Funeral Home. The kind lady who answered my eager inquiry was gentle with me, never once indicating her utter fatigue, in this three-college town, with yet another "Do-you-have-a-box-for-me?" call.

I have always been grateful for the friendly manner in which the McNutt Funeral Home let me down.

My mother's response to all this recollecting was, "Now, you shouldn't joke about something so serious," trying to hide a smile that progressed to a laugh. My wife, having heard my box-for-you story untold times, muttered something like, "Well, at least it'd give me more time for tennis."

Now, for those of you who insist on something serious, if not religious, in this corner, this is for you: if we can't joke about the most grim prospects concerning our lives, we're in bad shape indeed.

Such occasional joking helps put those somber events in perspective. It reminds us that no matter how valuable life is, its greatest worth is in those things that outlive us.

When one invests one's life in such as love and peace and truth and justice—and, yes, good humor, which surely is one of God's grandest gifts—one associates with things immortal.

So, never be surprised—or defeated—by the realization that some 222 number somewhere has a box for you. It's there, for all of us.

But just don't let that morbid realization cheat you out of having all the fun you can while you're still a-kickin'.

Afraid of Life

It's funny, in a way, to be afraid of life. But that's where I've been for the past several months.

Don't misunderstand me. It's not that I feel that life has been mean or unfair to me or that I'm mad at life or anything like that. It's quite the opposite.

I'm afraid of life because life is so good, so sweet. Life has been so grand these months—so grand that I've been scared that it might have something bad in store for me.

Do you know what I mean?

Those of you who've been sick, or who now may be, will best know what I mean.

If you've read the previous chapters, you know that about a year ago I learned I have cancer. (I inadvertently wrote, just now, "I learned I had cancer"—and that's really the way I feel about it; that I "had" it then, but not now. But I suppose there's a sense in which I should acknowledge that I just might still have cancer.)

That's the rub, of course. And that's why I've been so afraid of this sweet morsel called life—this marvelous, gorgeous gem; this firefly on a summer evening; this grand gift of new mornings and beautiful afternoons and peace-filled nights.

Illness, with the threat of its ultimate grim conclusion, can, if we allow it, take all that away from us.

So, though I enjoy life with a passion, I find myself in the strange position of being afraid of it.

There's good reason, of course. Months ago, my doctor told me that although such prognostications were inexact, there was a one-in-three chance that my cancer would reoccur.

I recalled that they also told me that the chances that I would have contracted this rare type of cancer —leiomyosarcoma—were about one in several million or so.

I also recalled that a couple of years before I learned I had cancer, I came down with another unusual ailment, which, the doctors said, was so rare that the chance of catching it was "about one in hundreds of thousands, probably millions."

I concluded that I could handle that one-in-three odds; it was those long shots that gave me trouble.

So here I am—in love with life, having a ball, and wanting to dance the night away.

It's funny about life. While all is going well, we don't give much thought to how sweet it is. That's natural, of course, and perhaps it should be. It would be morbid and a waste of time if we spent too much of life thinking about it rather than living it.

Another thing: no one lives forever. We all have to die. Some die young and healthy, others old and sick, and others a variety of combinations of the two.

As has been said, the real tragedy is not that so many die but that so many fail to really live. So many, rather than being properly afraid of life, are wrongly afraid of life—they fail to use it in fear of losing it (which is, in fact, what they accomplish by their fear).

So, Life, let's get on with it. I promise I won't let my fear become an obsession and that I won't allow it to become that "unhealthy" kind of fear.

And, oh yes. Promise me, Life, that we can dance like crazy till the music plays out.